Chring

J. Oswald Sanders

Christian Focus Publications

© 1977 J. Oswald Sanders Estate
ISBN 1 85792 060 0

This edition published in 1993
by
Christian Focus Publications Ltd
Geanies House, Fearn, Ross-shire,
IV20 1TW, Scotland, Great Britain.

Cover design
by
Donna Macleod

Cover illustration
by
Tricia Harrison

All rights reserved. No part of this publication may be reproduced, stored in a retrieval system, or transmitted, in any form or by any means, electronic, mechanical, photocopying, recording or otherwise, without the prior permission of Christian Focus Publications.

Unless otherwise indicated, biblical quotations are from the
New American Standard Bible
Copyright © The Lockman Foundation 1960, 1962, 1963, 1968, 1971, 1972, 1973.

AV = Authorised Version
RSV = Revised Standard Version
copyright 1946, 1952, © 1971, 1973 by the Division of Christian Education of the National Council of the Churches of Christ in the USA.

Printed and bound in Great Britain by
Cox & Wyman Ltd, Reading.

Contents

	Foreword	4
	Introduction	5
1.	Certainties of the Second Advent	7
2.	'I Shall Return'	10
3.	Why Must Christ Return?	17
4.	When Will Christ Return?	22
5.	How Will Christ Return?	26
6.	Signs of the Second Advent	30
7.	The Rapture of the Church	47
8.	The Blessed Hope of the Church	54
9.	The Great Tribulation	56
10.	Antichrists and the Antichrist	59
11.	The Millennium	66
12.	The Marriage Supper of the Lamb	71
13.	The Second Advent and the Judgement	76
14.	The Battle of Armageddon	87
15.	The Second Advent and Christian Doctrine	90
16.	The Second Advent and Missions	99
17.	What the Second Advent Will Mean to Christ	104
18.	What the Second Advent Will Mean to Us	107
19.	What the Second Advent Will Mean to Satan	110
20.	Practical Effects of the Doctrine	114
21.	Our Attitude to Christ's Return	118
22.	Heaven—Our Home	122

Foreword

This book highlights the leading truths that are linked with and dependent on the second coming of Christ. These are so clearly set out in Scripture that we can be absolutely sure of them, no matter which school of interpretation we follow.

The elements of speculation and sensationalism are excluded so that the essential truth of Scripture may more readily be seen. Popular assumptions which are not indisputably based on Scripture are avoided. Wherever possible the Scriptures are left to speak for themselves.

Where there is a divergence of views on any relevant point, the author has endeavoured to state the differing views fairly and objectively. So that the reader may see at a glance what Scripture has to say, the relevant biblical quotations are normally set out in smaller type.

It is the author's conviction that where there is agreement on the main elements of this doctrine, we should never allow differences of opinion on which godly men of all ages have been divided, to be a test of fellowship or an occasion of separation. Rather should they be an incentive to more diligent study of the Scriptures.

The author believes that it is of greater importance to stress the spiritual and ethical implications of the doctrine than to have an elaborate timetable of events. There is so much on which we are all agreed.

The objective throughout is eminently practical—not to gratify curiosity, but to stimulate holy living and motivate zealous Christian service.

Introduction

The aim of this study of the second advent of our Lord is to state clearly and with practical application those facts concerning this momentous event of which we can be absolutely certain, and on which most scholars of all schools of prophetic interpretation are agreed. This is done without any endeavour to fit these facts into any hard and fast scheme of prophetic interpretation. It is at this point that unprofitable controversy so often begins, and the blessing of 'the blessed hope' is lost.

In his *Commentary on Luke's Gospel* (p. 544), Norval Geldenhuys has this to say:

> As soon as attempts are made to draw up a programme of the future worked out in greater detail than is offered to us in God's Word, it causes discord and sectarian dissension. Clearly and gloriously, the Scripture presents the main facts with regard to the Savior's advent. What a mighty comfort lies in the prophesied facts, and what a tremendously urgent call that we should be vigilant and prepared.

One of the problems met by the student of the second coming of Christ, lies in the differing interpretations of the same passages of Scripture by equally godly Christian scholars. Furthermore, these views often seem contradictory to each other—especially in their interpretation of the highly symbolical book of the Revelation.

How are we to meet this problem? D. G. Stewart suggests this approach: 'I think it wise not to come to the study of this book in order to fit it into a pre-conceived plan and pattern, but to recognize that all schools of interpretation may have in fact some light to throw on God's Word.' (*The Reaper*, Institute Press 1966.)

As we approach our study of the relevant biblical passages, there are three questions that we should constantly have before our minds if we are to arrive at a satisfactory interpretation.

1. What did this passage mean to the people to whom it was written at that time?
2. What message does this passage have for me today?
3. What does this passage teach me about God's plan for coming days and ages?

The answer to these questions will throw a flood of light on the subject.

Many of us have been accustomed to one line of interpretation of the Scriptures relating to the second advent, and it is not easy for us to approach the subject with an open mind. Most of us tend to try to make every Scripture fit into our own preconceived scheme; but we should earnestly endeavour to adopt an objective approach, asking the Holy Spirit to enlighten our minds, and being willing to allow the views of other godly men to challenge our thinking.

It has been well said that the truth of the coming again of our Lord is revealed and unchangeable. Our theories of the fact are *not* inspired, and we ought not to be surprised to find that in some details they do not fully express the whole truth. To discover this and give up our theories is not to give up the truth, but to come to a fuller and richer appreciation of the truth.

It would be too much to expect that what is written will meet with full acceptance, but if the primary purpose of the book is achieved—to encourage believers to embrace and act upon the great certainties of the second coming of Christ—the author will be very happy.

J. Oswald Sanders

1
Certainties of the Second Advent

There are many things relating to the second advent of Christ of which *we can be absolutely certain*. There are other areas where the fundamental doctrines of Scripture are not involved, in which differences of interpretation by equally godly men call for loving tolerance.

'The importance of a doctrine may be judged somewhat by the proportionate space and prominence given to it in the New Testament. Measured by this standard, the theme of Christ's coming in glory is second to none in Scripture, not even the atonement, in the claim which it makes on our consideration.' (A. J. Gordon, *Behold He Cometh*, Thynne & Co. 1934, p. 11.)

Of all the certainties proclaimed in the Scriptures, none is so frequently mentioned, so clearly foretold and so forcefully applied as the fact that Jesus Christ will literally return to earth. And yet the fact remains that the second advent of Christ is a vital and stimulating hope to only a minority of Christians. To the early Christians His promised return afforded unwavering hope in the midst of fierce persecution. Christians meeting each other in the street used as their greeting, 'Maranatha'—'the Lord is coming'. To them the second advent was the joyous climax of God's eternal purpose.

'It is not crude, unintelligent fanaticism,' wrote Hugh Martin, 'to anticipate such a close to human history. There is no scientific reason to hold that the present material order of things on this planet will go on for ever. On the contrary, science seems to anticipate a time when earth will become uninhabitable. There is to be a day of reckoning, a Last Day, a Day of the Lord, a Day of Judgement. Belief in God involves a climax to the present stage of human history.'

However, it must be confessed that today the anticipated return of Christ is anything but a certainty to the majority of Christians. It is largely a neglected doctrine. How often, for example, does the reader have the opportunity of listening to a sermon on this subject? Many regard the whole concept with incredulity or amusement, and even among those who profess to believe it, instead of the joyous anticipation of our Lord's coming coronation, there often develops uncharitable controversy over details of interpretation. We must never allow details of interpretation to obscure or dim the glorious certainties.

C. S. Lewis regarded the second advent of Christ as an essential doctrine of the Christian faith, not as an optional extra. 'It seems impossible,' he said, 'to retain in any recognizable form our belief in the divinity of Christ and the truth of the Christian revelation, while abandoning, or even persistently neglecting the promised return of Christ.'

But having said this, it must be acknowledged that many passages of Scripture which promise or foretell the Lord's return, have in them an element of obscurity. The Lord intended it to be so. When He was on earth, He foretold certain happenings, but He gave this warning to His disciples: 'I am telling you before it comes to pass, so *that when it does occur, you may believe* that I am He' (Jn 13:19 italics mine). He was not foretelling these things merely to satisfy their curiosity, but in order that their faith might be strengthened and confirmed when the prophesied events came to pass. The implication is that they would understand the full significance of the prophecy only after it had been fulfilled. Then, like Peter, they would be able to say, 'This is what was spoken of

CERTAINTIES OF THE SECOND ADVENT

through the prophet.'

So is it with the events surrounding the second advent. Our Lord's own prophecies about His resurrection were not understood even by His own intimate disciples until that stupendous event had taken place. We must accept that many prophecies which are now difficult for us to understand and reconcile, will become clear only when the Lord comes. This should beget in us a due humility and deliver us from undue dogmatism.

As we approach our study, let us embrace and enjoy and concentrate on the clear light we do have on the subject—the certainties—and then we can expectantly await the further light the Holy Spirit will give in the foregleams of His approaching coming.

It needs no emphasis that the most important teaching on the second advent is that of the coming Lord Himself. Every other scriptural utterance on the subject must be interpreted in harmony with what He taught, and this invests His great prophetic utterance in Matthew 24 and 25 with tremendous importance. It is the seed plot, and every subsequent prophetic statement in the New Testament must be interpreted in the light of the specfic teaching of the final authority.

In addition to His great prophetic address, many of our Lord's parables had their focal point in His impending advent. Even the memorial supper was to be observed only until His return, and that event would mark the consummation of the age.

2
'I Shall Return'

We can be absolutely certain that our Lord Jesus Christ will come again as He promised.

During World War II General Douglas MacArthur, Commander of the American forces in the Far East, established his headquarters in the Philippines. At a time of crisis he was ordered by the United States Government to withdraw with his army from the Philippines. Knowing the probable tragic consequences to the Philippine nation of such action, he was most reluctant to do this, for during those dark days his presence and inspiring leadership had been deeply appreciated by the Filipinos. They had great confidence in him as a man of his word. But as he was leaving, he gave the dismayed nation his assurance, 'I shall return!' These three words from a man of undoubted honour whom they trusted implicitly, afforded desperately needed hope of ultimate deliverance to the beleaguered nation—a hope that later was fully realized.

On the dark night of our Lord's betrayal, in an intimate talk in the upper room, He opened His heart to His loved disciples and shared with them matters of deepest concern both to Him and to them. He began this moving discourse with words so unexpected, so mysterious, that it was only later that their vast significance began to dawn on his followers:

> I go to prepare a place for you. And if I go and prepare a place for you, *I will come again* and receive you to Myself;

that where I am, there you may be also.

> Jn 14:2-3 (italics mine)

'I am going away...I will come again.' These words, although only dimly understood at the time, were to afford un-dying hope to His countless followers throughout succeeding centuries.

How are we to understand these words? Did He mean that after His death His disciples would continue to experience His spiritual presence with them, or did He mean that He would literally return in person? In a few hours His disciples understood all too painfully the meaning of His words 'If I go...' for He died on the cross and later ascended into heaven before their astonished eyes. But what did He mean by the words, 'I will come again'? His 'going' is recorded in these words:

> And after He had said these things, He was lifted up while they were looking on, and a cloud received Him out of their sight.
>
> Acts 1:9

While the astounded disciples were gazing into the sky where He had disappeared, two heavenly messengers came and stood beside them, and gave the interpretation of Jesus' mysterious words, 'I will come again.'

> Men of Galilee, why do you stand looking into the sky? This Jesus, who has been taken up from you into heaven, will come in just the same way as you have watched Him go into heaven.
>
> Acts 1:11

Jesus' words and the interpretation given by the heavenly messengers are in clear and uncomplicated language. They indicate that the Christ who had risen from the dead and ascended into heaven would, at some future time, personally return from heaven to earth in some way similar to His departure.

There is no doubt about what these words meant to the disciples and the early Church. That great biblical scholar James Denney said, 'We cannot call in question what stands so plainly in the pages of the New Testament, what filled so exclusively the minds of early Christians—the idea of a personal return of Christ at the end of the age. If we are to retain any relation to the New Testament at all we must assert the personal return of Christ as Judge of all.' (Quoted in J. O. Sanders, *The Incomparable Christ*, Moody Press 1971, p. 249.)

Concerning the interpretation of the angelic message, another noted expositor, Alexander Maclaren, had this to say: 'He will come in like manner as He has gone. We are not to water down such words with anything short of a return precisely corresponding in its method to the departure: and as the departure was visible, corporeal, literal, personal and local, so too will be His return from heaven to earth, and He will come as He went, a visible manhood.'

If these two passages stood alone in the Scriptures, they would be sufficient to command and secure the belief of all who accept the Bible as the fully inspired Word of God. But far from standing alone, they are only two of the 318 times in which the second coming of Christ is specifically mentioned or referred to in the 210 chapters of the New Testament. This fact alone indicates the commanding importance of this theme to Christians of all ages, and warrants our giving earnest study to its meaning and implications.

But there are many sincere Christians who, for various reasons and in spite of the clarity of the New Testament teaching on the main features of this subject, are unwilling or unable to accept the fact that the Lord Jesus will return visibly and bodily. In support of their attitude they explain the relevant Scriptures in one of the following ways, all of which seem to the author equally unsatisfactory in adequately interpreting these passages.

The Lord comes at death

But does He? Does not Scripture teach rather that at death the believer departs to be with the Lord where He is? Hear Paul's words:

> But I am hard-pressed from both directions, having the desire *to depart* and be with Christ, for that is very much better.
>
> Phil 1:23

Actually the second coming of Christ is the opposite of His coming to the believer at death, for the Christians who have died rise from the dead at His coming.

> For the Lord Himself will descend from heaven with a shout...and the dead in Christ shall rise first. Then we who are alive and remain shall be caught up together with them in the clouds to meet the Lord in the air.
>
> 1 Thess 4: 16-17

To reveal the fallacy of this suggestion, one need only substitute the word 'death' for the Lord's coming in such passages as Titus 2:13, or the above Thessalonian passage. It reduces the passages to nonsense. In what conceivable way can 'death' be fitted into this picture?

> ...looking for the blessed hope and the appearing of the glory of our great God and Savior, Christ Jesus'
>
> Tit 2:13

Or consider this:

> Behold, He is coming with the clouds, and every eye will see Him, even those who pierced Him; and all the tribes of the earth will mourn over Him.
>
> Rev 1:7

To accept the explanation that Christ's second coming takes place at death is to confuse 'the last enemy' of the church with its 'blessed hope'.

The Lord came in the descent of the Holy Spirit at Pentecost

There is indeed a sense in which the descent of the Spirit at Pentecost could be called a coming of Christ, for He had plainly promised His disciples, 'I will not leave you orphans, I will come to you.' In the coming of the Holy Spirit, the disciples exchanged their Lord's bodily presence for His spiritual omnipresence. But this was not the fulfilment of the many passages foretelling the second coming of the Saviour in power and great glory.

Did Jesus not make it clear that the coming of the Holy Spirit was dependent, not on His *coming* but on His *withdrawal* from earth?

> But this He spoke of the Spirit, whom those who believed in Him were to receive; for the Spirit was not yet given, because Jesus was not yet glorified.
>
> Jn 7:39

At the time of Pentecost there was no New Testament, but many years later the writers of the New Testament treated the coming of Christ as an event still in the future. Further, in the recorded Pentecostal effusion, Jesus is seen at the right hand of God pouring out the Spirit:

> This Jesus God raised up again...Therefore having been exalted to the right hand of God, and having received from the Father the promise of the Holy Spirit, He has poured forth this which you both see and hear.
>
> Acts 2:32-33

So while Pentecost may in one sense be regarded as a coming of Christ to the Church, it is not the second coming of which Jesus and the apostles spoke and wrote.

The Lord came at the destruction of Jerusalem

It is true that in His great prophetic discourse in Matthew 24 and 25, Jesus did clearly foretell the destruction of Jerusalem which took place in AD 70. But it should be noted that in this passage Jesus nowhere indicated that this tragic and shattering event in which a million Jews were massacred, was identical with or would take place at the same time as His second coming.

It was after Jerusalem had been destroyed that John recorded these words of Jesus:

> Peter... said to Jesus, 'Lord, and what about this man [John]?' Jesus said to him, 'If I want him to remain until I come, what is that to you? You follow Me!'
>
> Jn 21:21-22

In this passage, the disciples obviously understood the Lord's reference to His coming to imply exemption from death. 'This saying therefore went out among the brethren that that disciple would not die' (v. 23).

In no sense could the destruction of the million Jews and the sack of Jerusalem be regarded as 'the blessed hope' of the Church.

In the light of the foregoing considerations, we need have no hesitation in believing that in keeping with His pledged word, the Lord Jesus will surely come again, not in weakness and humiliation as at His first advent, but in glory and power, for the final redemption of His Church and the judgement of the world.

It is worthy of note that the great creeds of the Christian Church have included the expectation of Christ's return. The Apostles' Creed declares that Christ 'ascended into heaven: and sitteth at the right hand of God the Father Almighty: from thence He shall come to judge the quick and the dead'. The Nicene Creed adds its witness: 'He shall come again with glory to judge both the quick and the dead.' The Athanasian Creed says, 'At whose coming all men shall rise again with their bodies and shall give account of their works.' These credal statements afford clear evidence that the second advent of Christ was an integral part of the Church's teaching.

The second coming of Christ also occupies a significant place in the great hymns of the Church, as for example, in Charles Wesley's vivid words:

> Lo! He comes with clouds descending,
>   Once for favoured sinners slain;
> Thousand thousand saints attending,
>   Swell the triumph of His train!
> Hallelujah! Hallelujah!
>   Jesus comes, and comes to reign.

3
Why Must Christ Return?

We can be absolutely certain that our Lord will return in order that the prophecies of Scripture might be fulfilled, His work of redemption completed and the world judged for its sin.

Are there compelling reasons for us to believe that Jesus will return to usher in the end of the age? Indeed there are.

1. He must return to fulfil His own promise. To one who accepts the Scriptures as the inspired Word of God, this is in itself an adequate reason, for 'He cannot deny Himself'. Could any promise be clearer or more definite than this?

> I go to prepare a place for you. And if I go and prepare a place for you, *I will come again* and receive you to Myself; that where I am, there you may be also.
>
> Jn 14:2-3

Some expositors link this prediction with verse 16 which refers to the coming of the Holy Spirit as Christ's personal representative. But as we saw in the last chapter, the coming of the Holy Spirit was dependent on Christ's departure from the earth, not His coming to it. (See Jn 7:37-39.)

There are many other passages in the Gospels in which our Lord's words can be interpreted only as His return in person to earth. For example:

Then the sign of the Son of Man will appear in the sky...
and they will see the Son of Man coming on the clouds of the
sky with power and great glory.

Mt 24:30

*2. He must return to complete the fulfilment of many Old
Testament prophecies concerning the coming of the
Messiah*, which were either fulfilled only partially, or
were totally unfulfilled.

One such prophecy is recorded in Luke 4:16-21. When
Jesus returned to His home town of Nazareth after the
wilderness temptation, He followed His normal custom
of attending the synagogue on the sabbath. He read the
set passage for the day, Isaiah 61. When He had read the
first half of verse 2, 'to proclaim the favorable year of
the Lord,' He closed the book, handed it back to the
attendant and said, 'Today this Scripture has been fulfilled in your hearing.'

Why did He stop reading in the middle of the verse?
Because while the first part of the prophecy was fulfilled
at His first coming, the terrible second part—'and the
day of vengeance of our God'—awaited its fulfilment
when He would return to earth at the end of the age. The
apostle Paul fills out this tragic picture:

The Lord Jesus shall be revealed from heaven with His
mighty angels in flaming fire, dealing out retribution to those
who do not know God and to those who do not obey the
gospel of our Lord Jesus.

2 Thess 1:7-8

*3. He must return to vindicate the statement of the two
heavenly messengers.* After the Lord had ascended into
heaven before the astonished gaze of His disciples, the
two men in white clothing assured them in the presence
of many witnesses that His departure from earth was not
for ever. He would return.

This Jesus, who has been taken up from you into heaven, will come in just the same way as you have watched Him go into heaven.

Acts 1:11

4. He must return to complete His work of redemption. His atoning work on the cross fully and for ever redeemed all who believe from the penalty and power of sin; but there is one aspect of redemption that still awaits completion. To Paul, redemption was incomplete without the redemption of the body.

We ... groan within ourselves, waiting eagerly for our adoption as sons, the redemption of our body.

Rom 8:23

At present we are 'at home in the body', but are 'absent from the Lord' (2 Cor 5:6). When Christ returns, body and spirit will be reunited (see 1 Thess 4:16-17). This is the ultimate goal of redemption.

5. He must return to confirm the truthfulness of Scripture. Every New Testament writer, without exception, bears witness to the return of Christ. Every book of the New Testament, with the exception of the small books of Philemon and 2 and 3 John makes reference to His second advent.

The apostle Paul writes twenty-seven times, sometimes at length concerning the second advent. In 1 and 2 Thessalonians it is mentioned in every chapter.

The writer of the letter to the Hebrews testified:

Christ also ... shall appear a second time, not to bear sin, to those who eagerly await Him, for salvation.

Heb 9:28

The apostle John affirmed it in unequivocal terms:

> We know that, when He appears, we shall be like Him, because we shall see Him just as He is. And every one who has this hope fixed on Him purifies himself.
>
> 1 Jn 3:2-3

> Behold, He is coming with the clouds, and every eye will see Him.
>
> Rev 1:7

James adds his witness:

> Be patient, therefore...until the coming of the Lord...for the coming of the Lord is at hand.
>
> Jas 5:7-8

Peter foretold conditions at the second advent:

> Know this first of all, that in the last days mockers will come...saying, 'Where is the promise of His coming? For ever since the fathers fell asleep, all continues just as it was from the beginning of creation.
>
> 2 Pet 3:3-4

Jude records Enoch's prediction, in the context of 'the judgement of the great day' (v. 6):

> And about these also Enoch, in the seventh generation from Adam, prophesied, saying, 'Behold, the Lord came with many thousands of His holy ones, to execute judgement upon all, and to convict all the ungodly of all their ungodly deeds which they have done in an ungodly way, and of all the harsh things which ungodly sinners have spoken against Him.'
>
> Jude 14-15

In the light of these and many other similar passages, the trustworthiness of the New Testament would be irreparably shaken if Christ failed to return.

6. He must return to execute judgement on those who have spurned His love and rejected His gospel.

> The Lord Jesus shall be revealed from heaven with His mighty angels in flaming fire, dealing out retribution to those who do not know God and to those who do not obey the gospel of our Lord Jesus. And these will pay the penalty of eternal destruction...when He comes to be glorified in His saints on that day.
>
> 2 Thess 1:7-10

7. He must return to answer the prayer He taught His disciples to pray:

> Pray, then, in this way...'Thy kingdom come.'
>
> Mt 6:9-10

4
When Will Christ Return?

We can be absolutely certain that no one knows exactly when Jesus Christ will come again.

While Scripture appears to teach that no millennium (a period of a thousand years of great blessedness on earth under Christ's rule) will occur before our Lord returns to receive His loved ones to Himself, the actual time of that return is not revealed. Indeed, He asserted that any attempt to fix its date was foredoomed to failure. It is a secret locked in the heart of the Father.

> But of that day and hour no one knows, not even the angels of heaven, nor the Son, but the Father alone.
>
> Mt 24:36

It should be noted that the phrase 'nor the Son' 'indicates that the perfect knowledge which all members of the Godhead share, was part of that which Jesus voluntarily refrained from using during His earthly ministry, except in those instances when such knowledge was necessary to His purpose' (*Wycliffe Bible Commentary* in loco). The statement is therefore to be understood as applying only to the days of His life on earth.

Just as there is an unmistakably definite revelation of the certainty of Christ's second coming ('The Lord Himself will descend from heaven with a shout...'), so there is an equally unmistakably definite revelation as to the time of that coming: 'Of that day and hour no one knows.'

This statement alone should be sufficient to discourage curious speculation on the subject, but through the years there have been repeated but futile attempts to fix the date, bringing resulting discredit on the truth itself. When Satan cannot keep a Christian back from grasping a biblical truth, it is his usual method to try to push him into an unbalanced viewpoint, as he did with the Thessalonian Christians (2 Thess 2:1-3).

'Every attempt that has been made to fix a date even approximately,' said Dr Campbell Morgan, 'has brought the truth into discredit, especially in view of the fact that many predictions have been made, and changed with startling adroitness, in order that the date might still further be postponed in view of previous mistakes.' (*Sunrise*, H. E. Walter 1964, p. 14) To see some contemporary event in every statement of the prophets will require revising one's views every ten years.

We must recognize that what God has revealed in the Bible is sufficient to satisfy faith, but it may not always be enough to gratify our carnal curiosity and desire for sensation. The New Testament was not written to satisfy those who are inquisitive about details of coming events, but to glorify the One who is coming, to stimulate faith in Him, and to strengthen believers for life and witness in a hostile world. Jesus made this very clear to His disciples before His ascension. In replying to their question, 'Lord, is it at this time You are restoring the kingdom to Israel?', He used strong words to rebuke their curiosity:

> It is not for you to know times or epochs which the Father has fixed by His own authority
>
> Acts 1:6-7

But while we do not know the exact time of the second advent, we do know, from Christ's teaching and that of the Holy Spirit through His apostles, the general character and conditions of the times in which He will come. To the unbelieving Pharisees who demanded of Him a sign to confirm His messianic claims, Jesus uttered a stern rebuke:

> When it is evening, you say, 'It will be fair weather, for the sky is red.' And in the morning, 'There will be a storm today, for the sky is red and threatening.' Do you know how to discern the appearance of the sky, but cannot discern the signs of the times?.
>
> Mt 16:2-3

This statement makes it clear that while the exact hour of His return is withheld from us, there will be clear 'signs of the times' which will enable the believer to recognize its approach. A 'sign' is an indication or happening by which a coming event may be recognized, and we are encouraged to be alert to detect them. It is for us, under the guidance of the Holy Spirit, to examine the happenings of our times in the light of the prophecies of Scripture.

There is a difference of opinion concerning the possibility of Christ returning at any time after He ascended. Some expositors hold that to the disciples and early Christians, the hope of the Church was that the Lord would return in their lifetime to receive them to Himself. They maintain that if certain events must intervene before He comes, it would have robbed those believers of their hope. To them the coming of the Lord has always been an any-moment coming.

Other expositors, however, hold that while today, because many prophesied events have been fulfilled, we may expect the Lord to return at any time, it was not so with the disciples and the early Church. They point out that Jesus foretold the gift and ministry of the Holy Spirit who would lead them into all truth and impart instruction He had not yet been able to give them (Jn 16:13). His ministry of conviction of sin, righteousness and judgement would continue over a period of time.

Jesus told Peter 'by what kind of death he would glorify God', using the words 'when you were younger' and 'when you grow old', so they maintain that John could not have been expecting the Lord to come in his lifetime (Jn 21:18-19; 2 Pet 1:14). Paul similarly expected death and not the second coming to end his life (2 Tim 4:6) and he warned the Ephesian Christians that after his departure 'savage wolves will come in among you, not sparing the flock' (Acts 20:29).

They also maintain that the fulfilling of our Lord's commission to take the gospel to the uttermost parts of the earth would necessitate a considerable period of time, and that in His parables of the second advent He frequently used the phrase 'after a long time'. In their view, although in the light of these Scriptures the early Christians were not encouraged to expect that the Lord would return immediately, this outlook did not quench or lessen for them the reality and beauty of the 'blessed hope' of the Lord's return.

This of necessity opens up the question, 'What did the early Christians mean by "the blessed hope" of Christ's second coming?' We will return to this question later.

5

How Will Christ Return?

We can be absolutely certain that our Lord will return to earth literally and personally at the end of the age.

As we contemplate this stupendous and mysterious event many questions spring to mind, not all of which will find an answer in the Scriptures. But our Lord and the apostles give very clear teaching concerning the 'how' of His second advent.

The following facts can be established from Scripture:

1. It will be a personal return. 'I will come' (Jn 14:3-4) 'I am coming quickly' (Rev 22:7). 'The Lord Himself will descend from heaven' (1 Thess 4:16). In referring to His return Jesus commonly used the term 'Son of Man', which especially emphasized His real humanity (e.g. Mt 24:30). The idea of a personal coming is prominent in the parables He used to illustrate His coming. In the parable of the ten virgins, for example, it is a real bridegroom who comes. The angels assured the watching disciples that He will be the very same person that ascended from the Mount of Olives, 'this Jesus' (Acts 1:11). Such statements leave us in no doubt as to the identity of the One who is coming.

2. It will be a literal return, since He 'will come in just the same way' as they had watched Him go into heaven (Acts 1:11). It will be as real and literal as His first coming. When they saw Jesus ascend into heaven with hands outstretched in blessing, it was no mere vision but a factual event. Those who are on earth when He returns will see Him 'descend from heaven' just as He ascended into heaven (1 Thess 4:16).

3. It will be an open and public return. In referring to 'false Christs', men who claimed to be the promised Messiah, Jesus said, 'If anyone says to you, "Behold, here is the Christ," or "There He is," do not believe him.... If therefore they say to you, "Behold, He is in the wilderness," do not go forth, or, "Behold, He is in the inner rooms," do not believe them. For just as the lightning comes from the east, and flashes even to the west, so shall the coming of the Son of Man be' (Mt 24:23, 26-27). His coming will be as open and public as the lightning flash. There will be no need to penetrate secret rooms or to go to the solitude of the desert to find Him.

4. It will be a visible return. It will be visible to the Church. 'We know that...we shall see Him just as He is' (1Jn 3:2). And it will be visible to the Jews and to the rest of the world. 'Behold, He is coming with the clouds, and every eye will see Him, even those who pierced Him; and all the tribes of the earth will mourn over Him' (Rev 1:7). Thus His coming will be universal in its effects.

5. It will be a sudden and dramatic coming. Christ's Kingdom will not come as the result of a leavening process in which the world gradually turns to Him in faith. It will come like a lightning flash, 'for just as the lightning comes from the east, and flashes even to the west, so shall the coming of the Son of Man be' (Mt 24:27). He warned His disciples to keep on the alert, 'lest he come suddenly and find you asleep' (Mk 13:36). Paul asserted that His advent would be 'in a moment, in the twinkling of an eye' (1 Cor 15:52).

6. *It will be an unexpected coming.* When Jesus came to earth the first time, He was not expected by the majority of His people, and it will be the same at His second coming. In warning His disciples to be ready and expectant, He gave as His reason: 'for the Son of Man is coming at an hour when you do not think He will' (Mt 24:44). As for the unbelieving world, 'While they are saying, "Peace and safety!" then destruction will come upon them suddenly' (1 Thess 5:3). Peter foretold that in the end time men will deny that He is coming again, advancing the argument that 'all continues just as it was from the beginning of creation'. They will jeer, 'Where is the promise of His coming?... But the day of the Lord will come like a thief'—and the visit of a thief is always unexpected —'in which the heavens will pass away with a roar and the elements will be destroyed with intense heat, and the earth and its works will be burned up' (2 Pet 3:4,10). And this was written two thousand years before the atomic bomb.

7. *It will be a glorious return.* The language employed by both the Lord Himself and His apostles to describe the second advent conveys the vivid impression of unparalleled majesty and glory.

> *With clouds*
> 'They will see the Son of Man coming on the clouds of the sky.'
>
> Mt 24:30
>
> 'Hereafter you shall see the Son of Man sitting at the right hand of Power, and coming on the clouds of heaven.'
>
> Mt 26:64
>
> 'Behold, He is coming with the clouds, and every eye will see Him.'
>
> Rev 1:7

> 'We who are alive and remain shall be caught up together with them in the clouds to meet the Lord in the air.'
>
> 1 Thess 4:17

In the Old Testament clouds frequently accompanied the manifestation of the divine presence (e.g. Ex 19:16; 40: 34-35), and the same phenomenon will characterize Christ's return.

With great power
In startling contrast to His first advent which was marked by the weakness of a tiny infant, He will come again in the full manifestation of His power.

> 'And then they shall see the Son of Man coming in clouds with great power and glory.'
>
> Mk 13:26

With great glory
> 'When the Son of Man comes in His glory...then He will sit on His glorious throne.'
>
> Mt 25:31

> '...when He comes in His glory, and the glory of the Father and of the holy angels.'
>
> Lk 9:26

The glory of God has been defined as 'the excellence, beauty, majesty, power and perfection of His total being'.

With angels
> 'The Son of Man is going to come in the glory of His Father with His angels.'
>
> Mt 16:27

While there will always remain an element of mystery as to the details of our Lord's coming, He has told us sufficient as to its manner to satisfy our faith, and to give us an unshakeable confidence that He is really coming again to take us to Himself and to reign in glory.

6
Signs of the Second Advent

We can be absolutely certain that there will be specific and clear signs which will intimate to us that the return of our Lord is near.

> Now learn the parable from the fig tree: when its branch has already become tender, and puts forth its leaves, you know that summer is near; even so you too, when you see all these things, recognize that He is near, right at the door.
>
> Mt 24:32-33

> And there will be signs in sun and moon and stars, and upon the earth dismay among nations, in perplexity at the roaring of the sea and the waves, men fainting from fear and the expectation of the things which are coming upon the world; for the powers of the heaven will be shaken.
>
> Lk 21:25-26

'Seeking for signs and their Biblical interpretation is a profoundly Christian eschatological attitude. It is the necessary by-product of the belief that this world is temporary, mortal, and destined to be swallowed up in a new transcendent Order, in which there shall be a *new* heaven and a *new* earth...Our Lord encourages His followers to seek for signs and to read their meaning, because it is these signs which herald His coming again to judge and triumph over the world. It is therefore our duty to understand all possible signs.' So wrote Dr D. R. Davies, the converted Communist scholar.

In His major prophetic message Jesus clearly distinguished between His actual coming in judgement and the time of trouble that would precede it.

> For many will come in My name, saying, 'I am the Christ,' and will mislead many. And you will be hearing of wars and rumors of wars; see that you are not frightened, for those things must take place, but that is not yet the end. For nation will rise against nation, and kingdom against kingdom, and in various places there will be famines and earthquakes. But all these things are merely the beginning of birth pangs. Then they will deliver you up to tribulation, and will kill you, and you will be hated by all nations on account of My name.
>
> Mt 24:5-9

The troubles and sorrows envisaged in this passage are not the end, but only the birth pangs that will precede the visible appearance in glory of the Son of Man. When we compare His predictions with the world events and trends of our own times, we have strong grounds for believing that we are entering upon the end phase of world history.

By a 'sign' we mean a mark or indication by which a coming event may be recognized and anticipated. We can tell by signs in nature that spring is coming, and Jesus leads us to believe that we can tell by the signs in the world when His second coming is drawing near.

What are some of the signs that would lead to this conclusion? It will be noted that the signs our Lord said would precede His coming were of a nature that are *likely to appear in every generation*—war, pestilence, famines, earthquakes. Because this is so, Christians throughout the centuries have held that the return of Christ was very near, for they saw the signs which they thought heralded the end.

It is true that these signs have been characteristic of many ages, but as one student of prophecy wrote: 'It is reasonable to suppose that signs will assume a greater magnitude as the time of the end draws near. Or at least they will appear in such proportions that the believers, for whom alone they are intended, cannot mistake in their presence and import, that the end of the age is near.'

We can expect that the essential characteristic of the age will remain the same to the end, but that at the end of the age the manifestations of evil will be more blatant, more shameless and intense.

We shall now consider some of these signs.

The political sign—*wars and rumours of wars*

> And when you hear of wars and rumors of wars, do not be frightened; those things must take place; but that is not yet the end. For nation will arise against nation, and kingdom against kingdom; there will be earthquakes in various places; there will also be famines. These things are merely the beginning of birth pangs.
>
> Mk 13:7-8

War has always plagued the world. Nations have always been hostile to other nations whom they have envied or feared; but a new factor in the end times will be the unprecedented intensity and universality of this sign of the second advent. Wars will be occurring all over the world at once.

We were promised that World War II would result in a world 'safe for democracy'. But the actual fact today is that never before have men lived in such a militaristic atmosphere, where fear is endemic. Every day, through newspapers, radio and TV, the sights and sounds of war echo in our ears. Since the atomic bomb, any horror and terror is within the bounds of possibility, and the devastating effects of war and violence become more ghastly every day. The frightening element in it all is that we have become so accustomed to its horrors that it makes little impression on our calloused emotions.

It is estimated that there have been 100 wars and major conflicts around the world since 1945. One authority asserted that about one quarter of the sovereign states on earth were engaged in inter-state or intra-state conflict involving the use of regular armed forces as the 1970s began.

In reviewing the history of past centuries, we can see one or two of these signs present at different times, but seldom if ever do we find all these signs actively present or on such a universal scale as they are in our day. When we see all of them in existence at one time, and to an unprecedented degree, we are justified in asking the question, 'Are we not witnessing the last turn of history's wheel?'

The 'natural' sign—*plagues and famines*

In addition to the sign of 'wars and rumors of war' we have the usual accompaniments of war, for each leads inexorably to the other:

> And there will be... in various places plagues and famines.
> Lk 21:11

UNO recently stated that apart from crops in the ground at that present time there were reserve supplies of food to meet world need for only three weeks. This fact should cause all thoughtful readers to think seriously. The spectre of famine is becoming increasingly familiar in many parts of the world. Two-thirds of mankind is undernourished, and thousands are dying every week as the result of famine conditions. With an expected increase in world population from the present four billion to seven billion by the year AD 2000, and the possibility of another billion being added every eight years, little imagination is needed to picture the possibilities that lie ahead. The battle to feed humanity will be one of the most pressing problems of the time.

In the *Reader's Digest* of June 1975 the following arresting assessment of the world food situation appeared:

> As many as 400 million people may be in peril of starving this year in Asia, Africa and Latin America, and there is no assurance that the situation will not worsen next year.
>
> The primary long-term factor responsible for the world food-crisis is the population explosion. The world is now increasing its population at the rate of 80 million a year. The human race did not reach its first billion until AD 1830. Only 100 years later, in 1930, the second billion was reached; 30 years later, in 1960, the third; and it took only 15 years for mankind to add the fourth....
>
> With some demographers predicting a population of 8 billion by the year 2000, those who deny the urgency of limiting the birth rate have to believe that somehow in the next 25 years we will be able to feed an additional population as large as that in the world just now.
>
> Yet, with thousands of years of effort behind us, we cannot even decently feed today's 4000 million people. ...At present rates, India will have another 207 million people by 1985....
>
> So far we are in a period of localized famines, but at any time there could be continent-wide catastrophes.

The social sign—
lawlessness, violence, immorality

Jesus portrayed the social, moral and ethical state of the world immediately prior to His return in graphic terms. There would be a repetition of the evils of the days of

Noah that precipitated the Flood. Earlier in this century it was believed that with the advance of education and science, the ideal society would gradually evolve. Everyone would have enough. But two disastrous wars and the worsening conditions of the present day have shattered that delightful mirage which had no basis in Scripture. The consensus of Scripture is that, as the reign of truth is gradually extended, so the power of evil will steadily expand towards the end.

> For the coming of the Son of Man will be just like the days of Noah. For as in those days which were before the flood they were eating and drinking, they were marrying and giving in marriage, until the day that Noah entered the ark, and they did not understand until the flood came and took them all away, so shall the coming of the Son of Man be.
>
> Mt 24:37-39

Words could not be clearer. The wickedness of man is approaching its zenith, and the inevitable day of judgement is on its way. As in Noah's day, people today are living just as if there were no God and no future.

Paul lists nineteen of the moral traits that will characterize the last days, every one of which is reflected in contemporary society. All nineteen could be matched with news paragraphs in our daily papers. Here they are:

> But realize this, that in the last days difficult times will come. For men will be lovers of self, lovers of money, boastful, arrogant, revilers, disobedient to parents, ungrateful, unholy, unloving, irreconcilable, malicious gossips, without self-control, brutal, haters of good, treacherous, reckless, conceited, lovers of pleasure rather than lovers of God; holding to a form of godliness, although they have denied its power; and avoid such men as these.
>
> 2 Tim 3:1-5

The contemporary decline in ethical standards and the shameless rebellion against all moral virtues has reached such shocking proportions that the more thoughtful even of those who are themselves caught up in the avalanche, fear where it will lead. Racial and other forms of violence are not only indulged in, but are glorified and given altogether disproportionate prominence in the news media. Industrial strife, hijackings, kidnappings and militant demonstrations are everyday fare and are taken as a matter of course.

Our age is shot through with lawlessness and rebellion. Indeed, it would not be too much to say that despite its vaunted advanced culture, ours is the most lawless age ever known. Fifty years ago Dr T. T. Shields described social conditions existing at the time in these words: 'There is rebellion against all authority, against every kind of restraint in the name of liberty. University professors plead for license; and the unit of society, the family, is being destroyed, the covenant of marriage nullified. Everywhere the principles of the decalogue are being called in question... There is no kind of human authority that can keep this rebellious world in order. (*Gospel Witness* 1935.)

One wonders what Dr Shields would write were he alive today!

The religious sign—*apostasy*

> And at that time many will fall away and will betray one another and hate one another. And many false prophets will arise, and will mislead many. And before lawlessness is increased, most people's love will grow cold. But the one who endures to the end, it is he who shall be saved.
>
> Mt 24:10-13

SIGNS OF THE SECOND ADVENT

Let no one in any way deceive you, for it will not come unless the apostasy comes first, and the man of lawlessness is revealed, the son of destruction.

2 Thess 2:3

Just as the first coming of Christ was preceded by a period of apostasy in Israel, so will His second coming be preceded by deepening apostasy in the Church. Paul assured the Thessalonian Christians that the day of the Lord and the rise of the Antichrist would not come until the final and great apostasy had taken place.

Apostasy is a falling away, an abandonment of faith in those who have known and professed it, a desertion and forsaking of God. Apostasy is anarchy in religion. In our day anarchy has invaded the realms of music, literature, art, morals and education, so it is not surprising that it should invade the realm of doctrine.

The apostasies of Israel in Old Testament times were pictured under the terms 'fornication' and 'harlotry' (see Hos 4:12; 5:3-4). The same figure of spiritual adultery is applied to apostates in the New Testament. James, our Lord's brother, addressed them as 'you adulteresses' (4:4).

Heresies and apostasies have distressed the Church from earliest times, but both our Lord and Paul foretold that they would reach their climax in the great apostasy which will prepare the way for the rule of the Antichrist. Jesus spoke of false Christs and false prophets arising, but warned His followers not to be misled.

Take heed that you be not misled; for many will come in My name, saying 'I am He,' and, 'The time is at hand'; do not go after them.

Lk 21:8

Paul warned Timothy that the time would come

> when they will not endure sound doctrine; but wanting to have their ears tickled, they will accumulate for themselves teachers in accordance to their own desires; and will turn away their ears from the truth, and will turn aside to myths.
> 2 Tim 4:3-4

Another feature of the apostasy will be the working of 'signs and false wonders'.

> Then that lawless one will be revealed... the one whose coming is in accord with the activity of Satan, with all power and signs and false wonders, and with all the deception of wickedness for those who perish, because they did not receive the love of the truth so as to be saved. And for this reason God will send upon them a deluding influence so that they might believe what is false....
> 2 Thess 2:8-11

One need only to study the condition of the Church in our day to be convinced that the apostasy is already here. As Jesus predicted, 'because lawlessness is increased most peoples' love will grow cold.'

The geological sign—*earthquakes*

> There will be great earthquakes.
> Lk 21:11

Earthquakes have occurred periodically down the centuries, but in our times the earth has trembled and been convulsed as never before in history. The number of destructive earthquakes occurring in the first half of this century was more than twice the number in the whole of the nineteenth century, and the number continues to increase. It is not merely that news travels more quickly today and that we have more accurate means of detection than in former times. Their occurrence is growing progressively more frequent and intense.

In addressing the British Association for the Advancement of Science in Leeds, the noted seismologist Professor Bailey Willis of Stanford University, USA, said that 'the Holy Land can expect to suffer earthquakes. A fault along which earthslides could occur, passes under the Mount of Olives.' (Quoted in Rene Pache, *The Return of Jesus Christ*, Moody Press 1955, p. 85.) This statement lends great significance to Zechariah's prophecy:

> And in that day His feet will stand on the Mount of Olives, which is in front of Jerusalem on the east: and the Mount of Olives will be split in its middle from east to west by a very large valley, so that half of the mountain will move toward the north and the other half toward the south. And you will flee by the valley of My mountains, for the valley of the mountains will reach to Azel; yes, you will flee just as you fled before the earthquake in the days of Uzziah king of Judah. Then the LORD, My God, will come, and all the holy ones with Him!
>
> Zech 14:4-5

The intellectual sign—*increased knowledge*

At the end of time...knowledge will increase.

Dan 12:4

These words of the prophet Daniel pinpoint one of the most amazing features of contemporary society. Never before have such tremendous strides been made in the realm of human knowledge and achievement. Who could have foreseen the triumphs of knowledge and invention that placed man on the moon? Who could have dreamed of the wonders of the heavens which have noe become commonplace pieces of knowledge to the children of today?

A few years ago it was estimated that the sum total of man's knowledge was doubling every ten years. Experts now estimate that it takes less than five years for man's store of knowledge to double. Throughout the world, more than one thousand new books are published every day. So vast has become the accumulated store of knowledge that it has been facetiously said that a specialist is 'a man who knows more and more about less and less'.

The demonic sign—*doctrines of demons*

> The Spirit explicitly says that in later times some will fall away from the faith, paying attention to deceitful spirits and doctrines of demons.
>
> 1 Tim 4:1

This warning from the Holy Spirit should cause us to expect in the end times a startling revival of demonic activity, and we are seeing this taking place on a worldwide scale. Just as our Lord's first advent sparked a great increase in demonic activity, so it will be in the days immediately preceding His second coming.

As the end draws near, it can be expected that the devil will intensify his efforts to wrest world dominion from Christ.

> Woe to the earth and the sea; because the devil has come down to you, having great wrath, knowing that he has only a short time.
>
> Rev 12:12

There can be no doubt that the incredible and terrifying increase in evil and crime of every sort is explained in part at least by the above verse. It explains the unprecedented upsurge of interest in the occult, the rise of innumerable spiritualist 'churches', and the growing cult of Satan-worship.

The economic sign—*unstable riches*

> Come now, you rich, weep and howl for your miseries which are coming upon you. Your riches have rotted.... Your gold and your silver have rusted. It is in the last days that you have stored up your treasure.
>
> Jas 5:1-3

World leaders today are largely preoccupied with and plagued by the economic and financial woes of our day. Never before has there been such widespread instability or such uncertainty as to whether there is really a panacea for the prevalent economic maladies of the world. Key words in the economic world are 'depression', 'recession', 'devaluation', 'inflation'. Experts flatly contradict each other both as to the cause and the cure of the present uncertainty. Thousands of millions of dollars are being lost on the stock exchanges overnight. What appeared to be financially sound institutions are suddenly crashing. Was this what James foresaw when he wrote the above words?

Scripture foretells that the existing economic and commercial systems are heading for total collapse, due as much to the tendencies working from within, as to the forces assailing them from without. This collapse is graphically predicted in the Revelation, where those who have grown rich through corrupt practices are represented as weeping and mourning over the loss of their temporal prosperity.

> And the fruit you long for has gone from you, and all things that were luxurious and splendid have passed away from you and men will no longer find them. The merchants of these things, who became rich from her, will stand at a distance because of the fear of her torment, weeping and mourning, saying, 'Woe, woe, the great city, she who was clothed in fine linen and purple and scarlet, and adorned with gold and precious stones and pearls; for in one hour such great wealth

has been laid waste!' And every shipmaster and every passenger and sailor, and as many as make their living by the sea, stood at a distance, and were crying out as they saw the smoke of her burning, saying, 'What city is like the great city?' And they threw dust on their heads and were crying out, weeping and mourning, saying, 'Woe, woe, the great city, in which all who had ships at sea became rich by her wealth, for in one hour she has been laid waste!'

Rev 18:14-19

The Palestine sign—*the Israeli nation*

Early in their history God warned His chosen people of the judgement that would befall them if they forsook Him and engaged in idolatry.

> When you become the father of children and children's children and have remained long in the land, and act corruptly, and make an idol in the form of anything, and do that which is evil in the sight of the Lord your God so as to provoke Him to anger...the Lord will scatter you among the peoples, and you shall be left few in number among the nations, where the Lord shall drive you. And there you will serve gods, the work of man's hands, wood and stone, which neither see nor hear nor eat nor smell.
>
> Deut 4:25, 27-28

The precise fulfilment of this prophecy is a matter of history. For 2,600 years the Jews were scattered among the nations of the world and endured indescribable sufferings. But in His mercy God inspired His prophets to give a message of hope to His suffering people, and promised that He would one day bring them back to their land.

> 'And I will be found by you,' declares the Lord, 'and I will restore your fortunes and will gather you from all the nations and from all the places where I have driven you,' declares the

SIGNS OF THE SECOND ADVENT

Lord, 'and I will bring you back to the place from which I sent you into exile.'

Jer 29:14

Then it will happen on that day that the Lord will again recover the second time with His hand the remnant of His people, who will remain, from Assyria, Egypt, Pathros, Cush, Elam, Shinar, Hamath, and from the islands of the sea. And He will lift up a standard for the nations, and will assemble the banished ones of Israel, and will gather the dispersed of Judah from the four corners of the earth.

Is 11:11-12

How remarkable is the fulfilment of these predictions in the last thirty years! In 1908 there were only 47,000 Jews in Palestine. Today there are more than three million who have come from more than one hundred different countries. This return to the Promised Land is the greatest since it was invaded by Nebuchadnezzar 2,500 years ago. Ezekiel's prophecy (36:33-35) that the barren desert would yet blossom as a rose, has been gloriously fulfilled.

The age-long Hebrew dream of a national home has at last been realized. Towards the end of the nineteenth century Dr Theodor Herzl launched the Zionist Movement, and the dream reached the first stage of its fulfilment when on 14th May 1948 Premier David Ben Gurion read the Declaration of Independence, announcing the establishment of a Jewish nation to be known as the State of Israel.

The existence of this tiny nation-state has from the first been strongly contested, and at the time of writing the Arab nations are no less determined than before to blot it out. The oil-rich Middle East with Palestine in the midst is still the sensitive and explosive nerve centre of international politics, and it is not difficult to envisage the great powers being drawn into the final conflict of the ages.

The miracle of the continued existence of the Jewish nation in spite of age-long dispersion, bitter persecution and near extermination is one of the wonders of the ages, and is not matched elsewhere in history. The Jew, though scattered among a hundred nations, has preserved his national identity and characteristics, and is unique. In the light of the Lord's return the significant factor is that these developments have all come to pass in the last few years.

The Jerusalem sign—*Gentile domination ended*

In His great prophetic discourse, Jesus made a double reference to the future of Jerusalem.

> But when you see Jerusalem surrounded by armies, then recognize that her desolation is at hand. Then let those who are in Judea flee to the mountains, and let those who are in the midst of the city depart, and let not those who are in the country enter the city....
>
> Lk 21:20-21

This prophecy was accurately fulfilled when the armies of Titus laid waste the city and massacred its inhabitants in AD 70. The Jewish historian Josephus records that in the terrible holocaust that resulted, 1,100,000 perished and 100,000 were carried away captive. Only because the Christians heeded the Lord's warning and fled from the doomed city during a lull in the fighting, were they spared the fate of those who stayed. They fled to Pella where they were safe from attack.

The second reference to Jerusalem reads.

> And they will fall by the edge of the sword, and will be led captive into all the nations; and Jerusalem will be trampled underfoot by the Gentiles until the times of the Gentiles be fulfilled.
>
> Lk 21:24

There is no space here for a discussion of the meaning of the phrase 'the times of the Gentiles'. The important fact to notice is that as a result of the Arab-Israeli Six Day War of 1967, for the first time in two millennia, Jerusalem was freed from Gentile control. The Arab nations are adamant in their determination to regain Jerusalem, but at the time of writing it is still firmly in Jewish hands and Israeli leaders are at one in saying that they will never give it up.

This could well be yet one more indication that we are at the end of 'the times of the Gentiles', and lead us to the conclusion that there is no reason why the Lord should not return at any time.

The evangelistic sign—
missions and mass media

Another sign which our Lord said would precede His coming was that of the universal proclamation of His gospel.

> And this gospel of the kingdom shall be preached in the whole world for a witness to all the nations, and then the end shall come.
>
> Mt 24:14
>
> The gospel must first be preached to all the nations.
>
> Mk 13:10

The implications of these statements are clear. Before the end, 'all the nations' must receive the witness of the gospel. There is no suggestion that all the nations will be converted, but they must all have the opportunity of hearing how they may be converted.

The technological discoveries of our day have made the fulfilment of this prophecy possible to a degree that could never before have been imagined. Today there is no nation in the world in which the gospel has not been preached, or in which there is no church, however weak and insignificant. However, this is far from saying that the world has been fully evangelized.

Radio has brought the gospel message to the ears of multiplied millions who could not otherwise have heard it. Gospel Recordings have brought the elements of the evangel to peoples of more than four thousand different languages and dialects. Improved translation techniques have resulted in more than 90% of the peoples of the world having at least a portion of the Scriptures in a language they can understand. The airplane has brought hitherto inaccessible parts of the world within easy reach of the missionary and his message.

Only God knows when this prophecy will reach its final and complete fulfilment, but it is beginning to appear as though we could say that the gospel has been preached for a witness to all the nations. Meanwhile, we must do all in our power through missionary endeavour to 'hasten on the day of the Lord'.

7
The Rapture of the Church

We can be absolutely certain that the Lord will return and will catch away His own children to be for ever with Him in glory.

The descent of the Lord from heaven to receive His own people to be for ever with Him, is popularly termed 'the rapture of the Church'. The English word 'rapture' is derived from the Latin *rapere* to transport from one place to another. It is not a Scripture term, but originates from an expression in Paul's first letter to the Thessalonians.

> For the Lord Himself will descend from heaven with a shout, with the voice of the archangel, and with the trumpet of God; and the dead in Christ shall rise first. Then we who are alive and remain shall be *caught up* together with them in the clouds to meet the Lord in the air, and thus we shall always be with the Lord.
>
> 1 Thess 4:16-17 (italics mine)

The rapture of the Church, then, refers to the catching up of the saints to meet the Lord in the air when He returns. Immediately after the resurrection that will take place at the sound of the archangel's voice and the trumpet of God (v. 16), Christians who are alive on earth will be changed, so that their bodies become immortal and incorruptible.

> Behold, I tell you a mystery; we shall not all sleep, but we shall all be changed, in a moment, in the twinkling of an eye,

at the last trumpet; for the trumpet will sound, and the dead will be raised imperishable, and we shall be changed.

1 Cor 15:51-52

Then the dead saints who have been raised and the living saints who have been raptured, will together ascend to meet their descending Lord, in whose presence they will dwell for ever.

But while we can be absolutely certain that the Lord will return and rapture His Church, and while there seems to be no reason why He should not now return at any moment, there is by no means agreement among students of prophecy concerning the nature and timing of the rapture.

The most commonly accepted view is the pre-millennial one. Most, though not all who hold this view—i.e. that Christ will return before the millennium—make a distinction between a coming of the Lord *for*, and His later coming *with* His saints; between His coming to catch up His saints to meet Him in the air, and their later return with Him to reign on the earth. The former event they term the 'rapture', and the latter the 'revelation' or 'appearing'. The rapture is secret to believers only; the revelation is public to the world. In between these two events, they believe the seventieth week of Daniel's prophecy (9:24-27) has its fulfilment, and the Great Tribulation takes place. They believe that the 'rapture' may take place at any moment, but that the 'revelation' will be preceded by a number of prophesied events, such as the judgement of the nations (Mt 25:31-46) and of the impenitent (Rev 20:11-15) and the establishment of Christ's Kingdom.

Many writers of the pre-millennial school lay stress on the usage of the Greek words *parousia* (presence) and *epiphaneia* (revelation). The first word is taken as referring to the coming of the Lord *for* His saints publicly in power and glory. But one prominent expositor of the pre-millennial view affirms: 'We conclude then, that from a study of the Greek words themselves, the coming of the Lord *for* His saints and *with* His saints, is not to be gleaned.' (C. L. Feinberg, *Pre-millennial or A-millennial?* p. 207.)

Those who do not follow the pre-millennial interpretation say that two crucial questions must be faced:
1. Does the New Testament teach a *secret* rapture of the Church? Is that event seen and heard only by believers and not by unbelievers who learn of it only through the disappearance of the Christians?

Objectors to this view hold that Scripture speaks only of a second coming, not of a second and a third coming, which seem to be involved in the two-stage theory. They point out that our Lord said the wheat and the tares would be together in the field until the harvest; but according to this view the wheat is removed at least seven years before the harvest and only tares are left. His promise was that He would return in the clouds of heaven with power and great glory, and would send out His angels to gather His elect; but according to this view He comes privately to take His people to Himself some years before His manifestation.

They also draw attention to the meaning of the words 'to meet' the Lord in the air (1 Thess 4:17). The expression occurs in the Greek in only two other places. In each case the person who is met continues to advance in the direction in which he was moving previously. This would imply where it is used in this verse, that the descending Lord is met by His saints, and He continues on His descent to earth with them after the meeting has taken place. The coming is not secret, but is preceded by 'a shout, the voice of the archangel and the trumpet of God' which 1 Corinthians 15:52 indicates will reach the dead.

While there is this divergence of viewpoint on the

secrecy of the rapture, there is absolute agreement on the *fact* of it, and those who hold the pre-millennial view will be found on both sides of the argument.

2. Does Scripture teach that before the Lord actually returns to earth, the raptured saints will dwell for a period with the Lord in the air, as is held by the pre-millennialist?

This would be a natural corollary to the idea of a secret rapture of the saints and a subsequent coming of the Lord to earth in power and glory. But objectors maintain that in 1 Thess 4:16-17, the key Scripture to the teaching on the rapture, there is no suggestion that the saints who are caught up will dwell for a period in the air. The purpose of the rapture, they maintain, is that they should meet the Lord in the air, not dwell with the Lord in the air. If Paul had meant to indicate that they would 'dwell with the Lord in the air', would he not have said so?

Prof. W. G. Moorehead, one of the original editors of the Scofield Bible and a pre-millennial scholar, is quoted in this connection: 'Christ does not return to heaven with His saints. He comes with them to the earth. As an ancient writer expresses it, "We shall be caught away to meet Christ, that all may come with Him to the battle."' (G. E. Ladd, *The Blessed Hope*, Eerdmans 1956, p. 50.)

Although there is this divergence of viewpoint as to the nature and timing of the rapture, let us not lose our grip on the glorious fact of it, or be censorious of those who hold a view different from our own.

Note on the use of *parousia, epiphaneia,* and *apokalupsis*

Three main words are used in the Greek language to describe the second coming of the Lord, the meaning of which it is important to understand.

The word most frequently used is *parousia*, which

occurs twenty-four times in the New Testament. Peter used it in reference to Christ's first coming, and this was certainly a historical event (2 Pet 1:16). While the basic idea of the word is 'presence', it means much more than that. 'It points to the coming that precedes the presence, or results in the presence' (Berkhof). It refers to a bodily rather than a spiritual presence. The word was applied to Paul:

> His letters are weighty and strong, but his personal presence is unimpressive.
>
> 2 Cor 10:10

When in olden times a king or emperor planned to visit a city, elaborate preparations were made, as in our day, for the 'parousia' of the important visitor. The early Christians were familiar with this use of the word, and employed it in that sense to describe the arrival of Christ as King of kings in power and glory.

'The *parousia* of Christ denotes His coming from heaven, which will be...a revelation of His glory, for the salvation of His Church, for vengeance on His enemies, for the overthrow of opposition raised against Himself, and finally to realize the plan of salvation.' (Cremer in the *Biblico-Theological Dictionary of New Testament Greek*, p. 234.)

We can take it that in every case where the term *parousia* is used, it refers to the coming of a person or a group, and this assures us that when our Lord returns it will be in 'the body of His glory' (See Mt 24:30; 25:31-34; Phil 3:21; 1 Thess 4:15-17; 2 Thess 2:1).

The second word is *epiphaneia*, the root meaning of which is 'appearance' or 'manifestation'. It carries with it the idea of brightness or splendour. The Greek-speaking people of Christ's day used to refer to the visit (*parousia*) of the emperor as the *epiphaneia* or manifestation of their imperial 'god and saviour', for this was how they regarded him. There was special emphasis on the thought that he was coming to help them. So the word has been defined as 'a visible manifestation of a hidden deity, either by personal appearance or by some deed of power'.

The picture behind the word is that of our Lord coming forth out of a hidden background, bringing with Him the blessings of full salvation. It carries the idea of meeting once again with someone who is already known.

> Looking for the blessed hope and the appearing [*epiphaneia*] of the glory of our great God and Savior, Christ Jesus; who gave Himself for us, that He might redeem us....
>
> Tit 2:13-14

The third word is *apokalupsis*, which means 'revelation' or 'unveiling'. Hence the Book of the Revelation is called 'the Apocalypse', because its central theme is the unveiling of Jesus Christ and the revelation of His power and glory. It is a term that 'points to the removal of that which now obstructs our vision of Christ'.

> ...to the degree that you share the sufferings of Christ, keep on rejoicing; so that also at the revelation [*apokalupsis*] of His glory, you may rejoice with exultation.
>
> 1 Pet 4:13

At the present time we can see the majesty and glories of our Lord only 'through a glass, dimly'. But these three words assure us that a day is coming when the veil will be removed from our eyes and when we will see God's glory in Christ unveiled.

> Therefore, gird your minds for action, keep sober in spirit, fix your hope completely on the grace to be brought to you at the revelation [*apokalupsis*] of Jesus Christ.
>
> 1 Pet 1:13

The three words represent three aspects of the great and majestic event. The Lord Himself will be personally present. He will appear to every eye, and He will be unveiled in all His glory.

> Be patient, therefore, brethren, until the coming [*parousia*] of the Lord.
>
> Jas 5:7

> Keep the commandment without stain or reproach, until the appearing [*epiphaneia*] of our Lord Jesus Christ.
>
> 1 Tim 6:14

> You are not lacking in any gift, awaiting eagerly the revelation [*apokalupsis*] of our Lord Jesus Christ.
>
> 1 Cor 1:7

8
The Blessed Hope of the Church

We can be absolutely certain that 'the blessed hope' of the Church of which Paul wrote, is the prospect of the appearing of our Lord Jesus Christ in glory and power.

> For the grace of God bringing salvation, appeared to all men, instructing us that denying impiety and worldly cravings, we should live discreetly...expectantly looking for the *blessed hope, even the appearing of the glory of our great God and the Saviour Jesus Christ.*
>
> Tit 2:11-13 (Wuest, italics mine)

As indicated earlier, there are differing conceptions of what is meant by the 'the blessed hope' of the Church in this verse. The viewpoint of the pre-millennialists, who believe that the Church will be raptured before the Great Tribulation, is stated by John F. Walvoord: 'For these believers [the Thessalonians] the rapture was an imminent hope, an event that would occur before the tremendous events prophesied in the Old Testament.... It is obvious that the comfort offered by Paul (1 Thess 4:18) had the prospect of immediate fulfilment, that the time of their separation from their loved ones could be short.' (*Armageddon,* Zondervan 1974, pp.187, 190.)

In the opinion of the pre-millennialists, this question is vital. How could the second advent be described as a blessed hope to believers if it is to be preceded by a time of great tribulation, or if certain events must first occur and 'a long time' elapse before the Lord returns? Does not its blessedness consist in the fact that He could return at any moment?

Those who do not subscribe to this view maintain, however, that this is what the Lord expected His followers to anticipate. He foretold a period of persecution ahead (Jn 15:18, 20; 16:2). He indicated that before He returned certain things must happen over a period of time (see Mt 24:9-12). They point out that both Peter and Paul knew they were going to experience death, and yet to both of them the prospect of the Lord's return was a vital and blessed hope. The fact that they knew it would not occur in their lifetime did not appear to dim it or rob it of moral and spiritual power.

The fact that Jesus told Peter 'by what death he would glorify God', they argue, must mean that to him the blessed hope was not the expectation of a secret rapture and escape from the great tribulation, but of some other aspect of Christ's coming. The fact that certain events and even death itself must intervene before Christ returned did not rob their hope of its blessedness.

If this contention is correct, it would seem that the blessed hope for which they were to look was something different from the prospect of an any-moment rapture. If so, in what did it consist? The blessed hope as they see it is the wonderful fact of the Lord's return and appearing in all His glory, and our union with Him at His coming—altogether apart from what might happen in the intervening period, be it long or short, or whether they escaped suffering or not. In Titus 2:13 Paul linked 'the blessed hope' not with a rapture at His 'parousia', but with His 'appearing' in glory at His 'epiphaneia'. The blessed hope in this view therefore includes all that the second coming will mean to the Lord, as well as what it means to us. Indeed, it is centred more on what it will mean to Christ and the fulfilment of His eternal purpose, than on what it will mean to us.

These are the alternative views between which the reader must choose.

9
The Great Tribulation

We can be absolutely certain that at the end of the age, and associated with the second coming of Christ, there will be a period of unprecedented tribulation and distress.

When you see the abomination of desolation which was spoken of through Daniel the prophet, standing in the holy place....then there will be a great tribulation, such as has not occurred since the beginning of the world until now, nor ever shall.

Mt 24:15, 21

But immediately after the tribulation of those days the sun will be darkened, and the moon will not give its light, and the stars will fall from the sky, and the powers of the heavens will be shaken, and then the sign of the Son of Man will appear in the sky, and then all the tribes of the earth will mourn, and they will see the Son of Man coming on the clouds of the sky with power and great glory.

Mt 24:29-30

And one of the elders answered, saying to me, 'These who are clothed in the white robes, who are they, and from where have they come?' And I said to him, 'My lord, you know.' And he said to me, 'These are the ones who come out of the great tribulation, and they have washed their robes and made them white in the blood of the Lamb.'

Rev 7:13-14

The great tribulation is generally thought to be 'the brief period of terrible judgements which immediately precedes the coming of Christ in His glory, coinciding with the reign of Antichrist' (*The Return of Jesus Christ*, p. 248). It is usually identified with Daniel's prophecy:

> And there will be a time of distress such as never occurred since there was a nation until that time; and at that time your people, everyone who is found written in the book, will be rescued.
>
> Dan 12:1

The Hebrew word for 'tribulation' has a large range of meanings in the Old Testament, but it usually signifies trouble of a general sort rather than of a special character. This is also true of the Greek equivalent in the New Testament, e.g. Mt 13:21; Jn 16:33.

Concerning the nature and time of this tribulation there has been a tremendous amount of controversy, much of it unfortunately negating the spirit of love.

H. Z. Cleveland in the *Zondervan Pictorial Bible Dictionary* (p. 871) states the three main views: 'The Great Tribulation is a definite period of suffering sent from God upon the earth to accomplish several purposes. According to *premillennial* eschatology it precedes the millennial reign of Christ. *Postmillennial* theology places it at the end of the thousand-year reign of Christ. *Amillennial* theology places it just before the new heavens and the new earth are brought in. This period of suffering will be unlike any other period in the past or future.'

Some expositors doubt whether the reference to 'a great tribulation' in Mt 24:21 can be identified with 'the great tribulation' of Rev 7:14 because Matthew links it with 'those in Judea' (v. 16). They see it fulfilled in the siege of Jerusalem in A.D. 70.

The intensity and extent of the divine judgement at this period may be gauged by the fact that one third of mankind will be killed.

> Authority was given to them over a fourth of the earth, to kill with sword and with famine and with pestilence and by the wild beasts of the earth.
>
> Rev 6:8
>
> A third of mankind was killed by these three plagues, by the fire and the smoke and the brimstone, which proceeded out of their mouths.
>
> Rev 9:18

The idea of such a holocaust would have seemed both incredible and impossible fifty years ago, but the nuclear age has placed in the hands of man an infinite capacity for self-destruction. Even secular literature recognizes such a dire possibility.

The judgements of God at this period will be supplemented by the malignance and wrath of His adversary the devil when he sees the imminence of his own defeat.

> Woe to the earth and the sea; because the devil has come down to you, having great wrath, knowing that he has only a short time.
>
> Rev 12:12

Whether or not the Church will pass through the tribulation is a much debated matter, each side claiming the support of Scripture for their position. This is one subject which the event itself will clarify, and probably not until then will there be unity of viewpoint.

10
Antichrists and the Antichrist

We can be absolutely certain that at the end of the age, the evil system fathered by the devil and referred to as 'the mystery of iniquity', will find embodiment in a towering and magnetic personality who will reduce the whole world to servitude and control it.

> Children, it is the last hour; and just as you heard that antichrist is coming, even now many antichrists have arisen; from this we know that it is the last hour.... Who is the liar but the one who denies that Jesus is the Christ? This is the antichrist, the one who denies the Father and the Son.
>
> 1 Jn 2:18, 22

> For many deceivers have gone out into the world, those who do not acknowledge Jesus Christ as coming in the flesh. This is the deceiver and the antichrist.
>
> 2 Jn 7

> Let no one in any way deceive you, for it will not come unless the apostasy comes first, and the man of lawlessness is revealed, the son of destruction, who opposes and exalts himself above every so-called god or object of worship, so that he takes his seat in the temple of God, displaying himself as being God.... And then that lawless one will be revealed whom the Lord will slay with the breath of His mouth and bring to an end by the appearance of His coming.
>
> 2 Thess 2:3-4, 8

The early Christians were united in the expectation that at the end of the age an evil and sinister figure with a powerful and magnetic personality would emerge and command universal attention. In writing to the Thessalonian Christians, Paul spoke of this personage as 'the lawless one', and the context indicates that he would be the product of the worldwide apostasy of which the Lord spoke in Mt 24:10-12. John referred to him as 'antichrist', and these two names, 'the lawless one' and 'antichrist', afford insight into his essential character.

The word 'antichrist' (against or instead of Christ), occurs only in the verses quoted above, but the basic idea is found frequently in Scripture. It may mean either 'the opposer of Christ' or 'the usurper of the names and rights of Christ'.

Person or system?

There has always been a difference of opinion among biblical scholars as to whether John is here speaking of an evil personage, or of an evil and pernicious system. Many have seen in the papacy the fulfilment of this prophecy. The answer is probably that he had both thoughts in mind, and that the evil person is but the personification and climax of the evil system, 'the mystery of iniquity' that is already at work in the world. In 2:18 John distinguishes between 'antichrist' and the 'many antichrists' that had arisen in the past. There are conditions in the world today that are preparing the way for the rule of the Antichrist.

Scripture speaks of 'the spirit of the antichrist' (1 Jn 4:3). It speaks of precursors of the antichrist: 'Even now many antichrists have arisen.' It speaks of the Antichrist himself: 'You have heard that Antichrist is coming.'

One of the early church fathers, Hilary, considered that 'the abomination of desolation' spoken of by the Lord in Mt 24:15 would have its fulfilment at the end of the world 'by the rise of a personal mighty Antichrist who would be worshipped by infidels'. It was Augustine's view that 'there can be no doubt that what is said here refers to the Antichrist and the day of judgement, or as Paul calls it, the day of the Lord'. So this is no new theory without a biblical or historical basis. Both Paul and John wrote in such a way as to show that the future emergence of the Antichrist was a teaching well-known at that time. 'Do you not remember,' Paul asked the Thessalonian believers, 'that while I was still with you, I was telling you these things?' (2 Thess 2:5)

We are therefore justified in believing that in the end times evil will become incarnate in a towering figure, the Antichrist, who will dominate the world scene. This mysterious and powerful person has been portrayed by Dr Rene Pache: 'He is the last great head to which the entire race will give itself at the end of time, and who will lead its ultimate revolt against the Lord and His Christ... This superman will incarnate all the power of Satan.' It is for us to satisfy ourselves that this conception is sustained by the relevant Scriptures.

The personality of the Antichrist

A significant statement in this connection was made by Lange, the great biblical scholar: 'Every idea ends in being incarnate in one of several individuals who thus becomes the perfect representative of it. If the Bible had not announced it, history would absolutely require an Antichrist who should come at the end of the time to press to the last limit the revolt of men against God.'

The same line of argument that theologians employ to demonstrate the personality of Christ or the Holy Spirit, may be used to establish that the Antichrist will be a real person. All that expresses personality is distinctly stated and expressly applied to him.

The entire description in 2 Thess 2:3-10 is of a personal character. Names are used of him that would apply only to a person: 'man of lawlessness', one who will not bow to authority; 'son of perdition', a term used of Judas Iscariot in Jn 17:12.

He performs actions that only a person can perform. He exalts himself, opposes God and all good, takes his seat in the temple of God, proclaims himself to be God. Like Christ he performs signs and wonders, but through demonic power. He, like Christ, has his 'parousia' and his 'epiphany'. He can be punished (Rev 20:10), and one can punish only a person, not a system.

It may have been this mysterious figure whom our Lord had in mind when He said to the Jews: 'I have come in My Father's name, and you do not receive Me; if another shall come in his own name, you will receive him' (Jn 5:43). Just as the Father achieved His purpose of blessing for the world through the personality of the Spirit-controlled Man, Christ Jesus, so Satan will employ a human personality over whom he has complete control, to attempt the overthrow of God and the ruin of His world. The godless world rejected the true Christ, but will welcome the Antichrist with open arms.

Christ and Antichrist

From what we have seen above, Christ and Antichrist stand in startling contrast in Scripture. Just as Jesus is the second Person in the holy Trinity of Father, Son and Holy Spirit (2 Cor 13:14), so the Antichrist is the second person of the diabolical trinity of the dragon, the beast and the false prophet (Rev 16:13). Jesus appears under the figure of a gentle Lamb (Rev 5:6), but the Antichrist as a ferocious beast (Rev 13:2). Christ humbled Himself; the antichrist exalts himself. Christ derived His authority direct from the Father (Mt 28:18); the Antichrist receives his authority direct from the devil (Rev 13:2). Christ performed His miracles for the glory of God; the Antichrist will perform miracles to draw attention to himself. Christ was the sinless man; the Antichrist is the man of sin. Christ's Bride is a church 'holy and blameless' (Eph 5:25-27); the bride of the Antichrist is a harlot, the apostate church (Rev 17:1ff).

The identity of the Antichrist

Through the ages there has been a great deal of speculation as to the actual identity of this coming superman, all of it fruitless. In this connection Dr Wilbur M. Smith writes: 'From the earliest apostolic writers down to this generation, Antichrist has been identified, but wrongly, with the Roman Empire, with Judas Iscariot raised from the dead, or Nero. The Reformers, even Luther and Calvin, identified Antichrist with the papacy, which is wrong. Many believed it was Napoleon Bonaparte, and in this century some said it was Mussolini or Hitler. All these guesses are wrong. We wait yet for the Antichrist to appear on the stage of history.' (*You Can Know the Future*, Gospel Light 1971, p. 49.)

Arnold Toynbee, the noted secular historian, had no problem in foreseeing emergence of such a figure as the result of the rise of technology and the breakdown of civilization. Here are his words: 'By forcing on mankind more and more lethal weapons, and at the same time making the world more and more interdependent economically, technology has brought mankind to such a degree of distress that we are ripe for the deifying of any new Caesar who might succeed in giving the world unity and peace.' (Quoted in Hal Lindsey, *The Late Great Planet Earth*, Lakeland 1971.)

The powers of the Antichrist

When he does emerge on the stage of world history, the Antichrist will assert his authority in three realms—

political, economic and religious.

He will exercise ruthless *political* control of the nations.

> And it was given to him to make war with the saints and to overcome them; and authority over every tribe and people and tongue and nation was given to him.
>
> Rev 13:7

He will maintain absolute *economic* control of the world.

> And he causes all...to be given a mark on their right hand, or on their forehead, and he provides that no one should be able to buy or to sell, except the one who has the mark....
>
> Rev 13:16-17

He will exert intolerable *religious* pressure on mankind to worship him as God, with the sole alternative of death.

> And there was given to him to give breath to the image of the beast, that the image of the beast might even speak and cause as many as do not worship the image of the beast to be killed.
>
> Rev 13:15

By this time the world will have reached such a condition of misery and political and economic chaos, that men will submit to and even welcome the iron rule of one who appears to bring the world back into control, and to restore some semblance of peace and security.

But their hopes are doomed to disappointment, for the period of his dominance is strictly limited.

> And there was given to him a mouth speaking arrogant words and blasphemies; and authority to act for forty-two months was given to him.
>
> Rev 13:5

The defeat of the Antichrist

Inevitably this brazen defiance of God reaches a climax in the confrontation of the forces of evil and the mighty power of God in what is commonly termed the battle of Armageddon.

> And I saw the beast and the kings of the earth and their armies, assembled to make war against Him who sat upon the horse, and against His army.
>
> Rev 19:19

Considering the stupendous issues at stake in this battle that will decide for ever the possession of the kingdoms of this world, the description is strangely brief. There is no long drawn-out conflict. It is supernaturally brought to an end. The imagery is vivid. The Lord will merely blow on the Antichrist and he is powerless, utterly defeated, and consigned to his eternal doom.

> And the beast was seized, and with him the false prophet who performed the signs in his presence, by which he deceived those who had received the mark of the beast and those who worshiped his image; these two were thrown alive into the lake of fire which burns with brimstone.
>
> Rev 19:20

11
The Millennium

One important point of interpretation on which there is a considerable divergence of opinion among equally godly, scholarly and evangelical Bible students, concerns what is called 'the millennium'. This word (from the Latin *mille annum*) means 'a thousand years', but does not actually appear in the Scriptures. The only passage where an actual time period of one thousand years occurs is in Rev 20:1-8. It is interesting to note that the idea of a millennial kingdom is not specifically found in the teaching of the Lord or His apostles, but it appeared early in the teaching of the Church.

The millennium is generally conceived to be a period of great blessedness on earth, with Jesus reigning on the throne of David in Jerusalem.

Dr J. O. Buswell has summed up the main views on the subject in the *Zondervan Pictorial Bible* (p. 534) in these words: 'Those who look for Christ's visible return preceding His millennial Kingdom, that is, pre-millenialists, adhere to the grammatico-historical method of exegesis, taking propositional truth in its simplest sense, understanding statements as 'literal' unless there is sound reason to believe them to be intended figuratively. On the other hand there has always been a tendency to 'spiritualize' or 'demythologize' whatever seems unfamiliar, and the interpretations of the millennium are numberless. Those called post-millennialists hold that Christ will return after the millennium. A-millennialists deny that there will be a millennial reign on earth.'

Post-millennial view

According to the post-millennial view, the second coming of Christ will follow the millennium. The Kingdom of God already in existence, is now being extended through the preaching of the gospel. The Church, like the leaven, will ultimately permeate the whole world, which will be Christianized, and know a period of universal brotherhood. At the close of the gospel dispensation there will be a millennial period of indefinite length, which will be succeeded by an outbreak of wickedness, culminating in a terrible conflict with the forces of evil at the coming of Christ. Simultaneously there will take place the resurrection of the dead and the final judgement.

It should be noted, however, that most of those who hold this view do not expect the Kingdom of God to be achieved on earth through human progress and social betterment, but rather by a supernatural process as a result of preaching the gospel.

But this picture hardly fits in with the parable of the wheat and tares, when both are said to grow together until the harvest at the end of the age. Nor does it match the harsh realities of the twentieth century. Two devastating wars within twenty-five years, the atomic bomb, and a rapidly worsening world outlook, lend little support to this view which is now largely out of favour.

Pre-millennial view

The pre-millennial view is the one most popular among evangelical Christians. Rev 20:1-8 is interpreted literally and it is believed that the Lord's second coming will usher in a millennium. Like the a-millennialists (non-millennialists), they anticipate a period of apostasy before the second advent. But they see the Lord's return not as a single coming, but as having two phases—His return *for* His people, and His return *with* His people.

In this view the Lord will come secretly, raise the dead saints, and catch them away with those believers who are alive on the earth, to be for ever with Him. This event is commonly known as 'the secret rapture'. This will be followed by a period of unprecedented tribulation and suffering—probably for seven years—during the latter half of which the Antichrist will rule the world. Believers will, they hold, escape this tribulation, having previously been caught away when the Lord comes in the air.

This period of tribulation will be followed seven years later by Christ's public coming in power and glory. The battle of Armageddon will be fought in Palestine, in which the Antichrist and the hosts of evil are utterly routed, and Christ will begin His reign on earth in Jerusalem. At the end of the thousand years Satan, who has been bound, will again be loosed and will stir up rebellion against the rule of Christ, who will defeat him and cast him and his associates into the lake of fire. This will synchronize with the resurrection of the wicked dead, and their final judgement at the great white throne. Then the eternal state will commence.

While this is briefly the generally accepted pre-millennial position, there are many who assent to the main features of this view but are not convinced that there will be a *secret* rapture or coming of the Lord, or that the Church will necessarily escape the sufferings of the tribulation period. They believe that Christ will come openly to take up His saints, overthrow the Antichrist, defeat the devil and establish His millennial Kingdom on earth. They do not conceive of His second advent as a two-stage event, for which they do not see scriptural support.

A-millennial view

Those who hold the a-millennial or non-millennial view

do not cherish the expectation of a glorious Kingdom of God on earth. They can discern no biblical ground for believing in a millennium before the Lord returns in glory and judgement. They interpret Rev 20:1-8 symbolically, and consider the millennial reign to be spiritual rather than earthly and temporal.

In their view the second coming of Christ will be preceded by widespread apostasy from the faith, culminating in the rise of the Antichrist. The Lord will crush this final rebellion at His coming, when He will raise believers who have died and take them together with all living saints to be for ever with Him. Simultaneously the wicked dead will be raised to face their final judgement. The earth will be overwhelmed in fire, and a new heaven and earth in which righteousness dwells will be brought into being.

This view is gaining considerable acceptance among evangelical Christians.

It is not the purpose of the author to advocate any particular view, but to state each fairly and to suggest books which advocate the different views, so that any reader who desires to proceed further with this study may do so.

In approaching research into this controversial area, it must be borne in mind that each of these views has been held and advocated by equally godly and scholarly men through the ages. *The important factor is that none of these views denies any fundamental truth of the Christian faith. The divergence is largely a matter of interpreting the timing of the events in the prophetic calendar, and on this point there is room for freedom of thought.* Unfortunately, our wily adversary has been all too successful in dividing believers over minor points of prophetic interpretation, and we have thus allowed him to gain the advantage. Let us resolutely refuse to fall into this snare, but allow to other Christians the same liberty of conscience as we would claim for our own interpretation. While they may differ among themselves, those who hold each of the above views are absolutely at one in their hope and conviction that Christ will come again, and one in their desire and determination to defend and propagate that central truth.

12
The Marriage Supper of the Lamb

We can be absolutely certain that Christ will return to be united for ever with the Bride chosen for Him by the Father.

This is the event for which all heaven is waiting—the union between Christ and His chosen bride. It is the event which the redeemed of every age have anticipated and longed for. It has formed the glowing predictions of the prophets and the songs of the Church, 'the era for which creation groans and the sons of God pray'.

The scene introducing the wedding opens with a great heavenly choir singing a hallelujah chorus. The song attributes glory and deliverance and power to God because of His righteous judgement upon the wicked and persecuting harlot-church (Rev 19:2-4). It is a song of rejoicing over the triumph of truth over error:

> And I heard, as it were, the voice of a great multitude and as the sound of many waters and as the sound of mighty peals of thunder, saying, 'Hallelujah! For the Lord our God, the Almighty, reigns.'
>
> Rev 19:6

Rejoicing that the Lord God Almighty has now revealed Himself in the full majesty of His power, the members of the heavenly chorus exhort each other to yet greater rejoicing.

'Let us rejoice and be glad and give the glory to Him, for the marriage of the Lamb has come and His bride has made herself ready.' And it was given to her to clothe herself in fine linen, bright and clean; for the fine linen is the righteous acts of the saints. And he said to me, 'Write, "Blessed are those who are invited to the marriage supper of the Lamb."' And he said to me, 'These are true words of God.'

Rev 19:7-9

To understand the symbolism of this sublime passage we require a background of knowledge of the marriage customs of the East. A Jewish betrothal was considered much more binding than an engagement is with those in western lands. The betrothed couple were to all intents and purposes looked upon as married. Infidelity during the period of betrothal resulted in divorce (see 2 Cor 11:2).

During the time that elapsed between betrothal and the marriage ceremony, the bridegroom paid the customary dowry to the father of the bride (see Gen 34:12). Then came the preparation and adornment of the bride who 'made herself ready' for the great event. In company with his friends, the bridegroom proceeded to her home, received her, and accompanied her to his own home or that of his parents. The climax was the solemn yet joyous marriage feast.

The imagery of marriage occurs frequently in both Old and New Testaments. Israel is often addressed as the bride of Jehovah (Is 54:6; Hos 2:14-20 etc.). Several of our Lord's parables centre around a wedding (Mt 22:2ff; 25:1ff; Mk 2:19-20). John the Baptist adopted the figure (Jn 3:29), as also did Paul (2 Cor 11:2; Eph 5:25ff).

Jesus is, of course, Himself the heavenly Bridegroom. The bride of whom John the Baptist spoke is obviously the true Church, which includes all who have exercised saving faith in Christ. The marriage symbolism expresses the indissoluble union of Christ and His redeemed people. But what of the devout Jews who believed under the Old Covenant? Are they included in the bride? Surely they are. Because they looked forward to the sacrifice of the Messiah, they shared in the salvation achieved by Christ (see Jn 8:56; Rom 3:25-26; 4:1-8). The Lord said that Abraham and Isaac and Jacob and all the prophets 'will recline at table in the Kingdom of God' (Lk 13: 28-29).

In Rev 21:12-14 it is indicated that the saints of Old Testament times will not be excluded from the festivities of the wedding feast.

> And one of the...angels...spoke with me, saying, 'Come here, I shall show you the bride, the wife of the Lamb.' And he...showed me the holy city, Jerusalem, coming down out of heaven from God.... It had a great and high wall, with twelve gates...and names were written on them, which are those of the twelve tribes of the sons of Israel.... And the wall of the city had twelve foundation stones, and on them were the twelve names of the twelve apostles of the Lamb.
>
> Rev 21:9-14

It would appear that the picture of the twenty-four elders seated on thrones in the presence of God confirms this interpretation.

Betrothal always has in view the wedding day, the happy climax to the growing intimacy and communion. The bride was chosen in Christ from all eternity. Christ's incarnation made possible her betrothal to Him. He paid the bride-price, the dowry, in crimson drops of precious blood at Calvary. Then came the interval until He comes to claim His bride and take her to the glorious home He has prepared for her. During this interval the bride makes herself ready.

> 'Let us rejoice and be glad and give the glory to Him, for the marriage of the Lamb has come and His bride has made herself ready.' And it was given to her to clothe herself in fine linen, bright and clean; for the fine linen is the righteous acts of the saints.
>
> Rev 19:7-8

Note that it was *given* or granted to her to clothe herself in fine linen. The wedding garments were customarily provided by the prince who gave the feast.

There is a diversity of opinion concerning the translation of 'the righteous acts of the saints' in v.8. Dr Leon Morris has this to say: 'This is usually understood in the sense of "the righteous deeds of the saints" (RSV). But the word *dikaioma* never seems elsewhere to have the meaning of "righteous deeds". It always denotes "ordinance" or something of the kind. "Sentence of justification" would be much more in accordance with New Testament usage. The plural will indicate that many individuals are involved. Such a meaning is demanded in this context by the verb *was granted*. The clothing is given to the saints. It is not provided by them. The white robes of the multitude in Rev 7:9, 14 were not provided by any righteous acts on the part of the wearers, but were the result of washing in "the blood of the Lamb". So it is here.' (*Revelation*, p. 227.)

The Bridegroom provides the wedding attire; the bride arrays herself in it.

If the translation 'the righteous deeds of the saints' is adopted, the only acceptable interpretation would be that we shall have to appear before God clothed in whatever righteous acts remain after the fire test spoken of in 1 Cor 3:12-15. This means that we cannot count on preparing ourselves for the marriage feast of the Lamb in the twinkling of an eye. It is here and now we are to produce works worthy of our heavenly Bridegroom.

Our Lord's two parables of the wedding feast underline two important truths in connection with the need of preparation for the coming of the Bridegroom. In the parable of the wedding garment it is the need of personal holiness. In the parable of the ten virgins it is the need of being filled with the Holy Spirit. We must be sure that we have received the wedding robe, and that our lamps are filled with oil.

The eastern wedding feast lasted for a week or sometimes for two weeks. The marriage supper of the Lamb lasts throughout eternity. A true marriage is a union for life. 'And thus we shall always be with the Lord' (1 Thess 4:17). The eternal union of Christ and His Church will be consummated in the home He has gone ahead to prepare for us.

13
The Second Advent and the Judgement

We can be absolutely certain that subsequent to the Lord's return, all believers will stand before the judgement seat of Christ, and all unbelievers will appear before the great white throne of judgement.

The second advent of our Lord cannot be separated from the thought of judgement, for it will precipitate the greatest series of judgemental events in the history of the world. He Himself foretold the resurrection of the just and of the unjust, to face the consequences of the deeds done in the body.

> Do not marvel at this: for an hour is coming, in which all who are in the tombs shall hear His [the Son of Man's] voice, and shall come forth; those who did the good deeds, to a resurrection of life, those who committed the evil deeds to a resurrection of judgement.
>
> Jn 5:28-29

Understandably, the concept of a coming judgement is the least popular article of the Christian faith, and is even denied by some claiming to be Christians. But it is a concept common to other religions and philosophies too. The Buddhist has his sixteen hells. The universal conscience of man testifies to a sense of guilt, a feeling of moral responsibility to a superior being or god to whom man is accountable, and who will reward good and punish evil. The distinctive feature of Christianity is that

God has committed his 'strange work of judgement' to His Son, Jesus Christ. It is He who will judge the living and the dead.

> For not even the Father judges any one, but He has given all judgement to the Son.
>
> Jn 5:22
>
> This is the One who has been appointed by God as Judge of the living and the dead.
>
> Acts 10:42

No one who accepts the authority of Christ and the authenticity of His words can doubt that there is a judgement to come. But there is a vast difference between the judgement of the believers and that of the impenitent. For the believer, there lies ahead the *bema* or judgement seat of Christ (2 Cor 5:10). For the impenitent there is the inescapable prospect of standing before 'the great white throne' of judgement (Rev 20:11).

It is neither possible nor necessary to fix an exact timetable for these great events—it is the certainty of them that is important. We must remember that when they take place, the measures of time and space with which we are familiar will be over and have no relevance. But speaking in terms with which we are familiar, would it not be reasonable to conclude that since 'the day of salvation' has extended over two millennia, we need not necessarily compress 'the day of judgement' into a brief period? But does this judgement require a long time as we know it? It is a well-known fact that in an hour of crisis, the whole of a life has been flashed before the mind of the subject in a moment of time.

Let us consider first the judgement of believers.

The judgement seat of Christ

One of the most important events connected with the Lord's return so far as believers are concerned is the fact that Christ will then ascend His judgement seat, and we must all appear before Him.

> But you, why do you judge your brother? Or you again, why do you regard your brother with contempt? For we shall all stand before the judgement seat of God. For it is written, 'As I live, says the Lord, every knee shall bow to Me, and every tongue shall give praise to God.'
>
> Rom 14:10-11

> Therefore do not go on passing judgement before the time, but wait until the Lord comes who will both bring to light the things hidden in the darkness and disclose the motives of men's hearts; and then each man's praise will come to him from God.
>
> 1 Cor 4:5

> For we must all appear before the judgement seat of Christ, that each one may be recompensed for his deeds in the body, according to what he has done, whether good or bad.
>
> 2 Cor 5:10

Does this mean that we will have to wait until that day to know whether we will be saved or lost? Does Scripture not teach that upon believing in Christ we pass from death to life, and shall not come into the judgement?

Indeed it does! The explanation lies in the fact that Scripture recognizes two kinds of judgement. There is the judgement where the *judge* in criminal proceedings sits on his bench, hears the evidence and decides the guilt and condemnation or the acquittal of the person charged. Then there is the judgement of the *umpire* who, as at the ancient Olympic Games, ascends his judgement seat to pronounce the winner and award the prize because the winner has run fairly and well. Those who have not run fairly and well suffer loss and receive no prize.

It is this second judgement seat that Paul has in view in the above verses. Rom 14:10 does not contradict 8:1 which asserts, 'There is therefore now no condemnation [or judgement] for those who are in Christ Jesus.' The passages quoted above have nothing whatever to do with being saved or lost, but are concerned solely with rewards for the faithful believer or loss for one who has been unfaithful. Man's eternal destiny is already determined in this life according to whether or not he has trusted Christ for salvation.

Few verses of Scripture are more soul-searching than Rom 14:12.

> So then each one of us shall give account of himself to God.

The noted American statesman Daniel Webster, on being asked what was the greatest thought he had ever entertained, replied, 'The greatest thought that has ever entered my mind is that one day I will have to stand before a holy God and give an account of my life.'

The judgement seat of Christ, then, is His 'umpire seat' and the purpose of the judgement is to assess and reward believers for the way in which they have used their opportunities and discharged their responsibilities. The basis on which we will be judged is clearly stated:

> We must all appear before the judgement seat of Christ, that each one may be recompensed *for his deeds in the body, according to what he has done, whether good or bad.*
>
> 2 Cor 5:10 (italics mine)

In his first letter to the Corinthians Paul had counselled them:

> Do not go on passing judgement before the time, but wait until the Lord comes who will both bring to light the things

hidden in the darkness and disclose the motives of men's hearts.

> 1 Cor 4:5

Christ's judgement and awards will therefore take into account not only our deeds (what we have done with our privileges and opportunities) but also our motives (why we have done it). It is the motive that imparts quality to an action.

Paul tells us how this judgement will be carried out:

> No man can lay a foundation other than the one which is laid, which is Jesus Christ. Now if any man builds upon the foundation with gold, silver, precious stones, wood, hay, straw, each man's work will become evident...because it is to be revealed with fire; and the fire itself will test the quality of each man's work. If any man's work...remains, he shall receive a reward. If any man's work is burned up, he shall suffer loss; but he himself shall be saved, yet so as through fire.
>
> 1 Cor 3:11-15

This passage suggests that there is a difference between sonship and reward; that there can be a saved soul but a lost life because of unfaithfulness in the stewardship of life.

In view of the serious possibilities implicit in this passage, it will be worthwhile reviewing what constitutes the 'gold, silver and precious stones' in this pictorial passage:

Our testimony to Christ
Holding fast the word of life, so that in the day of Christ I may have cause to glory because I did not run in vain nor toil in vain.

> Phil 2:16

THE SECOND ADVENT AND THE JUDGEMENT

Our suffering for Christ
But to the degree that you share the sufferings of Christ, keep on rejoicing; so that also at the revelation of His glory, you may rejoice with exultation.

1 Pet 4:13

Our faithfulness to Christ
Who then is the faithful and sensible steward, whom his master will put in charge of his servants, to give them their rations at the proper time? Blessed is that slave whom his master finds so doing when he comes.

Lk 12:42-43

Be faithful unto death, and I will give you the crown of life.

Rev 2:10

Our service for Christ
Now he who plants and he who waters are one; but each will receive his own reward according to his own labor.

1 Cor 3:8

For God is not unjust so as to forget your work and the love which you have shown toward His name, in having ministered...to the saints.

Heb 6:10

Our generosity to Christ
Now this I say, he who sows sparingly shall also reap sparingly; and he who sows bountifully shall also reap bountifully.

2 Cor 9:6

Instruct those who are rich in this present world not to...fix their hope on the uncertainty of riches, but on God.... Instruct them...to be generous and ready to share, storing up for themselves the treasure of a good foundation for the future....

1 Tim 6:17-19

Our use of time for Christ
Therefore be careful how you walk...making the most of your time, because the days are evil.

Eph 5:15-16

Conduct yourselves with wisdom toward outsiders, buying up the favourable time.

Col 4:5 (margin)

Our exercise of spiritual gifts for Christ
As each one has received a special gift, employ it in serving one another, as good stewards of the manifold grace of God.

1Pet 4:10

It is just like a man about to go on a journey, who called his own slaves, and entrusted his possessions to them. And to one he gave five talents, to another, two, and to another, one, each according to his own ability....the one who had received the five talents went and traded with them, and gained five more talents.... But he who received the one talent went away...and hid his master's money. Now after a long time the master of those slaves came and settled accounts with them. And the one who had received the five talents came up and brought five more talents.... His master said to him, 'Well done, good and faithful slave...I will put you in charge of many things....' And the one... who had received the one talent came up and said, 'Master.... I was afraid...and hid your talent in the ground; see, you have what is yours.' But his master...said.... 'take away the talent from him, and give it to the one who has the ten talents.'

Mt 25:14-28

Our self-discipline for Christ
Those who run in a race all run, but only one receives the prize. Run in such a way that you may win. And everyone who competes in the games exercises self-control in all things. They...do it to receive a perishable wreath, but we an imperishable.

1 Cor 9:24-25

Our winning souls for Christ
For who is our hope or joy or crown of exultation? Is it not even you, in the presence of our Lord Jesus at His coming?

1 Thess 2:19

THE SECOND ADVENT AND THE JUDGEMENT

The awards conferred by our Lord from His umpire seat are referred to under the figure of crowns—like the laurel crown won at the Olympic or Corinthian Games. For the disciplined and self-controlled believer there is *'an incorruptible crown'* (1 Cor 9:25 AV). For the saint who joyously and successfully endures temptation there is the *crown of life* (Jas 1:12-13: Rev 2:10) For the faithful servant who loves the appearing of the Saviour there is the *crown of righteousness*. For the winner of souls there is the *crown of rejoicing* (1 Thess 2:19-20 AV). For the zealous and faithful pastor and preacher of the word there is the unfading *crown of glory* (1 Pet 5:2-4).

But the judgement seat of Christ is not all joy and awarding prizes. Paul told the Corinthians that just as the stars differ in glory, so also will the saints (1 Cor 15:41-42).

Some will be ashamed when He comes because of unfaithfulness to Christ, of persistence in known sin, or having been ashamed of Him before men.

> And now, little children, abide in Him, so that when He appears, we may have confidence and not shrink away from Him in shame at His coming.
>
> 1 Jn 2:28

Some will suffer loss because they have used wood, hay and straw in building on the foundation, and these materials cannot withstand fire. As F. E. Marsh has said, 'They have built the material of earth's products upon the foundation of Christ's being and work. The gold of Christ's deity, the silver of His vicarious sacrifice, and the precious stones of His peerless worth and coming glory, are truths that will stand the test of God's fire; but the wood of self-esteem, the hay of man's frailty and the straw of human eloquence will all be burnt up, although the worker himself will be saved.'

> If any man's work is burned up, he shall suffer loss; but he himself shall be saved, yet so as through fire.
>
> 1 Cor 3:15

Will we be among those who receive the full reward and have an abundant entrance into Christ's Kingdom, or will we be among those who are ashamed and suffer loss?

Now let us turn to the judgement of the impenitent.

The great white throne

> And I saw a great white throne and Him who sat upon it, from whose presence earth and heaven fled away, and no place was found for them. And I saw the dead, the great and the small, standing before the throne, and the books were opened; and another book was opened, which is the book of life; and the dead were judged from the things which were written in the books, according to their deeds. And the sea gave up the dead which were in it, and death and Hades gave up the dead which were in them; and they were judged, every one of them according to their deeds.
>
> Rev 20:11-13

No more solemn and awe-inspiring scene is to be found in the whole of the Bible. In a few vivid sentences John portrays the scene determining the eternal destiny of the impenitent of all ages.

He saw in a vision a great white throne, its whiteness expressing the divine glory and holy justice of the One who sat upon it, the Lord Jesus Christ. It has been well said that so stupendous is the task of justly deciding the destiny of the incalculable numbers of beings involved, with all the intricate, complicated and secret factors that interact in each life, that no mind less than that of God Himself could be equal to the task. But of course Jesus Christ is God, and is perfectly qualified to be the arbiter of man's destiny.

The 'dead' mentioned in this passage are 'the rest of the dead' who had no part in the first resurrection (20:5), and this includes the unregenerate of all ages. The basis of their judgement is according to the 'deeds done in the body', as they are recorded in the 'books' of verse 12. It is sobering to think that a record of all our deeds exists. But is it not true that it is we ourselves who are compiling the record? Each of us is the author of his own life story.

The 'other book' (v. 12) is the 'book of life', in which the names of the redeemed are inscribed. If anyone's name is not written in this book, the record of his deeds in the other books condemns him to the lake of fire. Only those whose names are written in the book of life are safe from the sentence of condemnation.

> And death and Hades were thrown into the lake of fire. This is the second death, the lake of fire. And if anyone's name was not found written in the book of life, he was thrown into the lake of fire.
>
> Rev 20:14-15

Although this description is highly figurative, it none the less represents terrible and tragic realities. If it is contended that the fire and brimstone cannot be material, for it is not material forms that are cast into it, and material fire does not hurt spirit beings, that does not detract from the solemnity of the picture. As G. H. Lang has said, 'There must be agents as potent to hurt the spirit form as fire and brimstone to torment the body; and the nature of the figure used, a lake, suggests that the element is fluid, penetrating, enclosing, inescapable, fearfully adapted to its required purpose.' (*The Revelation of Jesus Christ*, p. 353.)

Just as there will be degrees of reward for believers, so will there be degrees of punishment for the impenitent. It will be 'more tolerable' for some than for others according to the degree of light enjoyed.

The prospect of the great white throne is so terrible that it should cause every thinking unconverted man or woman to seek the salvation from this judgement which Christ so freely offers.

There are those expositors who see the judgement seat of Christ and the great white throne not as two separated events, but as two aspects of the same event; one as it affects believers, and the other as it affects unbelievers. Whether this is so or not does not affect the validity of what is written above.

14

The Battle of Armageddon

We can be absolutely certain that at the end of the age there will be a vast confrontation between the evil trinity —the beast, the devil and the false prophet—and the victorious Christ who will finally and for ever crush them and secure their final doom.

Despite the fact that the word 'Armageddon' appears only once in Scripture, it has found its way into everyday speech and has become a popular synonym for a universal and probably final conflict at the end of the age. The *Oxford English Dictionary* defines it as 'the place of the last decisive battle at the day of judgement, hence used illustratively for any final conflict on a great scale'.

The relevant Scripture passage reads:

> ...they are spirits of demons, performing signs, which go out to the kings of the whole world, to gather them together for the war of the great day of God, the Almighty. (Behold, I am coming like a thief. Blessed is the one who stays awake and keeps his garments, lest he walk about naked and men see his shame.) And they gathered them together to the place which in Hebrew is called Har-Magedon.
>
> Rev 16:14-16

The nature of the conflict is given in Rev 19:19.

> And I saw the beast and the kings of the earth and their armies, assembled to make war against Him who sat upon the horse, and against His army.

Megiddo was a fortress town situated at the head of a mountain pass which led to the coastal plain, and on a hill overlooking the main road through the Plain of Megiddo. The Plain of Megiddo is triangular in shape, the sides measuring roughly fourteen miles, twenty-four miles, and fourteen miles.

Today Megiddo is a quiet pastoral place, but some of the greatest battles of history have been fought there, battles that have decisively influenced the entire course of world history. Over the centuries it has been conquered by Egyptians, Canaanites, Israelites, Philistines, Assyrians, Greeks, and Romans. In 1918 General Allenby defeated the Turkish armies and led the Allied forces through the Megiddo Pass, thus saving the Near East for the Western Allies. With this geographical and historical background, how appropriate it is that this plain is represented as the focus of the final battle of the ages.

Opinions differ as to whether this culminating conflict between the massed forces of evil and the forces of righteousness is fought on the literal site of Har-Magedon. Some believe that this small plain, only twenty-four miles long, would be far too small to stage a battle on a modern scale, at which 'the kings of the whole world' are gathered together. They view the events recorded in Rev 16:14-16 as symbolic of the final conflict between rebellious man and Almighty God, a conflict which is inevitable, whatever its nature.

Whatever may be in doubt about this great event, certain things are clear and on these points all evangelicals are agreed:

(a) There is going to be a final and universal confrontation between the forces of evil under the leadership of Satan and the Antichrist, and God and His hosts. Intimations of this age-end battle are found in Joel 3:9-15 and Zeph 3:8.

(b) The battle is not one in which physical armaments and military strategy will decide the issue. Nor will it be a long drawn-out conflict.

(c) Christ, as King of kings and Lord of lords, will crush the final rebellion and vanquish all His enemies by His dazzling appearance in glory, accompanied by His saints and the armies of heaven.

> And I saw the beast and the kings of the earth and their armies, assembled to make war against Him who sat upon the horse, and against His army. And the beast was seized, and with him the false prophet...these two were thrown alive into the lake of fire which burns with brimstone. And the rest were killed with the sword which came from the mouth of Him who sat upon the horse....
>
> Rev 19:19-21

> And then that lawless one will be revealed whom the Lord will slay with the breath of His mouth and bring to an end by the appearance of His coming.
>
> 2 Thess 2:8

So the beast (the leader of anti-Christian persecution), and the false prophet (the leader of anti-Christian religion and philosophy), together with the devil (the arch-criminal of the universe), are effectively crushed, and God's victory is complete.

In his book *More than Conquerors* (Tyndale Press 1947, p. 196) W. Hendriksen makes this comment: 'Har-Magedon is the symbol of every battle in which, when the need is greatest and believers are oppressed, the Lord suddenly reveals His power in the interests of His distressed people and defeats the enemy.... When the world, under the leadership of Satan, antichristian government, antichristian religion—the dragon, the beast and the false prophet—is gathered against the church for the final battle, and the need is greatest; when God's children, oppressed on every side, cry for help; then suddenly, dramatically, Christ will appear to deliver His people. That final tribulation, and that appearance of Christ on the clouds of glory to deliver His people, that is Har-Magedon.'

15
The Second Advent and Christian Doctrine

We can be absolutely certain that because the doctrine of the second coming of Christ is accorded such a significant place in the realm of Christian doctrine, God intended that it should have an equally prominent place in our preaching and teaching.

A preacher friend of the author once told him that he had just concluded preaching a series of messages on the second coming of Christ which had been attended by much blessing. In his study of the subject he discovered that this theme was linked with many of the great doctrines of Scripture, a striking evidence of the centrality of this important truth in the scheme of God. He therefore took up in succession the great doctrines of the Bible, and expounded them in their relation to the coming of Christ.

Since this theme is so prominent in the realm of Christian doctrine, should it not be equally prominent in our thinking and in our teaching?

Let us pass a selection of these doctrines in brief review.

The deity of Christ

When Jesus was challenged by the high priest to declare whether or not He was the Son of God, His reply was to assert His second coming to earth—this time not in humiliation, but in power and glory:

'I adjure You by the living God, that You tell us whether You are...the Son of God.' Jesus said to him,'...hereafter you shall see the Son of Man sitting at the right hand of Power, and coming on the clouds of heaven.'

Mt 26:63-64

Resurrection

It is stated in Scripture that those who have died 'in Christ', that is, those who are believers, will be raised from the dead when Christ returns. Then they will receive their resurrection bodies which will be suited to their new environment.

> But now Christ has been raised from the dead, the first fruits of those who are asleep....as in Adam all die, so also in Christ all shall be made alive. But each in his own order: Christ the first fruits, after that those who are Christ's at His coming.
>
> 1 Cor 15:20-23

Sanctification

In his letters to the Thessalonian church, Paul twice urges this blessed hope as a powerful incentive to sanctification and holy living.

> May the Lord cause you to increase and abound in love for one another, and for all men...so that He may establish your hearts unblamable in holiness before our God and Father at the coming of our Lord Jesus with all His saints.
>
> 1 Thess 3:12-13

Hope

The Lord's return is presented in Scripture as the ground and foundation of the Christian's hope. Without doubt the hope of the Church throughout the early centuries was the hope of Christ's glorious return. It stimulated them in service and sustained them in time of trial.

> Looking for the blessed hope and the appearing of the glory of our great God and Savior, Christ Jesus.
>
> Tit 2:13

Service

In the parable of the pounds (Lk 19:11-27) Jesus illustrated three truths: (1) He was going away; (2) He would return; (3) when He returned, He would appropriately reward His servants for their diligence in His service. He expected them to trade with the gifts, talents and opportunities entrusted to them, and His anticipated return would be a powerful incentive to diligence and faithfulness.

> He went on to tell a parable, because...they supposed that the kingdom of God was going to appear immediately.... 'A certain nobleman went to a distant country to receive a kingdom for himself, and then return. And he called ten of his slaves, and gave them ten minas, and said to them, "Do business with this until I come back."'
>
> Lk 19:11-13

Patience

Six times in six verses, James exhorts the much-tried believers to whom he is writing to show patience and endurance in most difficult circumstances. For them the outlook was dark and forbidding, but James counsels them to look upwards to the advent of their Lord, the hope of whose coming would strengthen them to endure.

> Be patient, therefore, brethren, until the coming of the Lord. Behold, the farmer waits for the precious produce of the soil,

being patient about it, until it gets the early and late rains. You too be patient; strengthen your hearts, for the coming of the Lord is at hand.

Jas 5:7-8

Watchfulness

In the midst of the seductions and allurements of a decadent and godless world, an eager expectation of and longing for Christ's return will provide both defence and protection from the devil's wiles.

> Therefore be on the alert, for you do not know which day your Lord is coming.
>
> Mt 24:42

Fidelity

Faithfulness in the discharge of entrusted service and in maintaining doctrinal purity is highly commended by the Lord, and will be amply rewarded. Paul obviously believed that the prospect of the appearing of the Lord in glory would encourage faithfulness in believers when tempted to slackness or indolence, or when the going was hard.

> I charge you in the presence of God...that you keep the commandment without stain or reproach, until the appearing of our Lord Jesus Christ, which He will bring about at the proper time.
>
> 1 Tim 6:13-15

Godliness

The second advent of the Lord will be associated with world-shaking events, culminating in the destruction of the present heavens and earth as we know them. The anticipation of these terrible judgements on a lawless world should produce in believers true godliness and holy conduct. In the nuclear age the possibility of such a holocaust is no longer unbelievable.

> But the day of the Lord will come like a thief, in which the heavens will pass away with a roar and the elements will be destroyed with intense heat, and the earth and its works will be burned up. Since all these things are to be destroyed in this way, what sort of person ought you to be in holy conduct and godliness, looking for and hastening the coming of the day of God, on account of which the heavens will be destroyed by burning, and the elements will melt with intense heat!
>
> 2 Pet 3:10-12

Separation

Believers are called upon to walk a pathway of separation from the world, which Jesus said hated Him before it hated them. Anticipation of 'the blessed hope' will help to achieve this.

> For the grace of God has appeared, bringing salvation to all men, instructing us to deny ungodliness and worldly desires and to live sensibly, righteously and godly in the present age, looking for the blessed hope and the appearing of the glory of our great God and Savior, Christ Jesus....
>
> Tit 2:11-13

Sonship

In his first letter, John the apostle affirms that believers are indeed now the children of God. But he links the attainment of complete family-likeness to their heavenly Father with the coming of the Lord.

> Beloved, now we are children of God, and it has not appeared as yet what we shall be. We know that, when He appears, we shall be like Him, because we shall see Him just as He is.
>
> 1 Jn 3:2

Sincerity

In several of his letters Paul exhorts the believers to whom he writes, to aim at sincerity of mind and attitude and blamelessness of character. The prospect of the coming of the day of Jesus Christ would inspire them to this end.

> And this I pray...that you may approve the things that are excellent, in order to be sincere and blameless until the day of Christ.
>
> Phil 1:9-10

Comfort

Is any truth more calculated to bring comfort to the lonely or bereaved than that of our Lord's promised return?

> Let not your heart be troubled.... I go to prepare a place for you.... And...I will come again, and receive you to Myself; that where I am, there you may be also.
>
> Jn 14:1-3

> The Lord Himself will descend from heaven...and the dead in Christ shall rise first. Then we who are alive and remain shall be caught up together with them in the clouds to meet the Lord in the air, and thus we shall always be with the Lord. Therefore comfort one another with these words.
>
> 1 Thess 4:16-18

Reward

When Paul had all but reached the finishing tape in his earthly race, he shared with young Timothy his unshakeable assurance of a worthy reward, not for himself alone, but for all who love his Lord's appearing.

> I have finished the course, I have kept the faith; in the future there is laid up for me the crown of righteousness, which the Lord, the righteous Judge, will award to me on that day; and not only to me, but also to all who have loved His appearing.
> 2 Tim 4:7-8

Pastoral diligence

Peter doubtless had the memory of his humbling interview with his Master in mind when he counselled the elders of the Church to faithfulness and diligence in the discharge of their pastoral functions. A sense of accountability to the Chief Pastor will provide a needed stimulus.

> Shepherd the flock of God among you...voluntarily...with eagerness...proving to be examples to the flock. And when the Chief Shepherd appears, you will receive the unfading crown of glory.
> 1 Pet 5:2-4

Rejoicing in trial

Jesus and His apostles were at one in their teaching that tribulation and suffering would be the lot of faithful believers while they were in a hostile world. But the prospect of the coming glory of the Son of God, in which they would be partners, would enable them to rejoice even in the midst of fierce persecution and suffering. Many of the martyrs proved the truth of Peter's words:

Beloved, do not be surprised at the fiery ordeal among you, which comes upon you for your testing, as though some strange thing were happening to you; but to the degree that you share the sufferings of Christ, keep on rejoicing; so that also at the revelation of His glory, you may rejoice with exultation.

1 Pet 4:12-13

Church attendance

Belief that Christ may return at an hour we do not expect, should have an effect even on the regularity of our attendance at church and fellowship meetings.

Not forsaking our own assembling together, as is the habit of some, but encouraging one another; and all the more, as you see the day drawing near.

Heb 10:25

Ministry of the Word

Both Paul and Peter stress the influence that the teaching of the second advent of Christ should have on the teaching and preaching of the Word of God. Many contemporary preachers testify to a transformation of their ministry when they have restored this doctrine to the place of importance given to it in Scripture.

I solemnly charge you in the presence of God and of Christ Jesus, who is to judge the living and the dead, and by His appearing and His kingdom: preach the word; be ready in season and out of season; reprove, rebuke, exhort, with great patience and instruction.

2 Tim 4:1-2

Premature judgement

Because we are fallible and do not know all the facts and factors involved in any situation, we are enjoined not to indulge in premature judgement and criticism of the actions of our brethren, but to reserve our judgement until the omniscient Lord comes.

> Therefore do not go on passing judgment before the time, but wait until the Lord comes who will both bring to light the things hidden in the darkness and disclose the motives of men's hearts; and then each man's praise will come to him from God.
>
> 1 Cor 4:5

16

The Second Advent and Missions

We can be absolutely certain that the Lord will return when the gospel has been preached for a witness to all nations.

The eleven disciples were eagerly discussing the future of their land. They were intensely interested in a revival of the independence and glory of their nation, and were speculating on what would be the next event in God's prophetic programme. 'Lord, is it at this time You are restoring the kingdom to Israel?' they asked (Acts 1:6). How wonderful it would be for the nation if the galling Roman yoke were struck from their shoulders. No longer would they be an occupied and a subjugated country, smarting under the humiliation of the oppressor!

But the heart of Jesus was not concerned with visions of national revival for Israel. It was bursting with a passionate desire for the salvation of the lost world for which He had just poured out His blood. Small wonder that He was dismayed at their absorption in dreams of worldly glory. His stern reply recalled them to the path of duty. Not Jewish aggrandizement but world evangelism was His consuming concern.

> It is not for you to know times or epochs which the Father has fixed by His own authority; but you shall receive power when the Holy Spirit has come upon you; and you shall be My witnesses... even to the remotest part of the earth.
>
> Acts 1:7-8

These words enshrine the supreme objective of the Church, and they have lost none of their relevance in our time. Not preoccupation with material prosperity and enjoyment, not unholy curiosity about coming events, not a selfish desire to escape the tribulations that might lie ahead, but a passion to carry the gospel to every creature. This is the charter of the Church. Is it our passion, or are we preoccupied with worldly interests?

There are certain Scriptures that appear to teach that our Lord made His return conditional on the Church's obedience to His command to evangelize the world.

> And this gospel of the kingdom shall be preached in the whole world for a witness to all the nations, and then the end shall come.
>
> Mt 24:14

In the same connection Mark says:

> The gospel must first be preached to all the nations.
>
> Mk 13:10

In the light of these verses, is it not reasonable to assume that since Christ has not yet returned, it is, in part at least, because the supreme task entrusted to the Church has not been completed? Is the Lord delaying His coming until His Church obeys His last command?

In his second letter, the apostle Peter implies that the time of Christ's return is not so inflexibly fixed that the Church cannot hasten it on by more rapid worldwide evangelism. The staggering thought is that each believer can do something to hasten the Lord's return. By implication we are either hastening it on or hindering it. Let us not keep our heavenly Bridegroom waiting.

> Since all these things are to be destroyed in this way, what sort of people ought you to be in holy conduct and godliness, looking for and hastening the coming of the day of God?
>
> 2 Pet 3:11-12

> Let all that look for, hasten
> That coming glorious day,
> By earnest consecration
> To walk the narrow way;
> By gathering in the lost ones
> For whom the Lord did die
> In the crowning day that's coming
>   By and by.

To the objection that this would make Christ's return dependent on man's effort rather than on God's sovereign grace, it can be replied that God in His sovereignty has always made use of men and earthly factors in the accomplishment of His purposes. It has been suggested that God does not necessarily reckon time arbitrarily as we do, in terms of days and months and years, but perhaps in terms of conditions and developments which make for the fulfilment of the plans He has in mind.

God foresaw the disobedience of the Church in failing to fulfil His commission, and the apparent delay of His Son's second advent, but the promise was not invalidated.

> The Lord is not slow about His promise.... But the day of the Lord will come like a thief....
>
> 2 Pet 3:9-10

If the foregoing presumptions are true, it would seem that the Lord made His advent contingent on three things:

1. *There must be some degree of readiness on the part of the Church.*

> The marriage of the Lamb has come and His bride has made herself ready.
>
> Rev 19:7

> When He appears, we shall be like Him.... And every one who has this hope fixed on Him purifies himself, just as He is pure.
>
> 1 Jn 3:2-3

It should be noted that it is the activity of the bride that is in view here, not the action of God. There is something for the believer to do in anticipation of the Bridegroom's return. Whatever else these verses may mean, it is clear that there is to be a purging and purifying of the Church before Christ returns.

2. *The Church must be complete,* for Christ will not be united to an incomplete bride.

> I looked, and behold, a great multitude, which no one could count, from every nation and all tribes and peoples and tongues, standing before the throne and before the Lamb, clothed in white robes.
>
> Rev 7:9

To the Holy Spirit was entrusted the task of finding a bride for Christ, and He has been faithful to His trust. When our Lord's earthly ministry came to its close, He reported to His Father, 'I have accomplished the work which Thou hast given me to do.' On the fulfilment of His task the Holy Spirit will give a similar report, but as yet He cannot do so, for He awaits the Church's full cooperation and obedience. The bride of Christ must be completely representative of humanity.

3. *The Church must have finished her task.* Can we say that this has yet been done? Thank God it can be said with confidence that there has never been a day when this has been more nearly accomplished. No less a missionary authority than Dr K. S. Latourette asserts that today Christianity is more widely distributed, more

deeply planted, more closely united, and exerting a wider and more vital influence than ever before in history. But as our Lord has not yet returned, the implication is clear that the task is not yet completed.

Writing in the *Alliance Weekly,* that great missionary statesman Dr Robert A. Jaffray said, 'I am convinced that the one thing of first importance for which the Lord is waiting ere He can return is the preaching of the gospel to every nation of the world as a witness. This must be done in order to bring back the King.'

The last stone has yet to be laid in the heavenly building. The last soul has still to be won. Could it be that my little piece of service, my tiny contribution to the missionary task may be the last thing required to bring in that soul and thus hasten the second advent? Peter urges us to eagerly look, and diligently work to speed on that advent.

What a powerful incentive this should be to more intense and earnest missionary endeavour. It proved to be so to Dr Hudson Taylor. 'If the Lord is coming soon, is it not a very practical motive for greater missionary effort?' he wrote. 'I know of no other that has been so stimulating to myself.'

Charles R. Erdman of Princeton Theological Seminary has said, 'In spite of all differences and disturbances, the work of His followers is to be pressed. Their task is clear. Until it has been completed, the King will not return. Whatever differences of opinion may exist among the servants of the King relative to details of His return, all should be united in the accomplishment of their common task and inspired by the same blessed hope.' (Quoted in G. E. Ladd, *The Blessed Hope,* p. 149.)

But is it not a stark tragedy that while we can joyously look for and anticipate our Lord's second advent, so great a proportion of the world's population still waits to hear of His first advent?

17
What the Second Advent Will Mean to Christ

We can be absolutely certain that Christ's second coming will mean much more to Him than it does to any of us.

The inherent selfishness of even the regenerate heart is revealed by our tendency to think of our Lord's second coming more in terms of what it will mean to us—how the accompanying events will affect us—than of what it will mean to Him. We are thrilled at the thought of our inheritance in Christ, but are we equally thrilled at the thought of what 'His inheritance in the saints' (Eph 1:18) means to Him? Is He indifferent to it? Do we give sufficient thought to His eager expectation of His coronation day, His wedding day?

> He is waiting with long patience
>   For His crowning day,
> For that Kingdom which shall never
>   Pass away
> Waiting till His royal banner
>   Floateth far and wide,
> Till He seeth of His travail,
>   Satisfied.

Consider the startling contrasts between His first advent and His second advent. Then He came in poverty and humiliation; now He comes with incredible riches and glory. Then He came in weakness; now He comes in power. Then He came to loneliness; now He is accompanied by His angels and the company of the redeemed. Then He came as a Man of sorrows; now He comes with radiant and unalloyed joy. Then in mockery men placed a reed in His hand; now He takes up and wields the sceptre of the universe. Then men placed a crown of acanthus thorn on His brow; now He comes adorned with the many diadems He has won. Then He was blasphemed, denied, betrayed; now every knee bows to Him, acknowledging Him as King of kings and Lord of lords.

When Jesus prayed His high-priestly prayer just before His passion, He made only one request of His Father, a request that unveiled the deep yearning of His heart.

> Father, I desire that they also, whom Thou has given Me, be with Me where I am, in order that they may behold My glory, which Thou hast given Me.
>
> Jn 17:24

When He comes again this earnest desire will have its fulfilment, and 'so shall we ever be with the Lord'. He will be fully satisfied with the outcome of His costly sacrifice, for 'He shall see of the travail of His soul, and shall be satisfied' (Is 53:11 AV). He will then experience the consummation of 'the joy set before Him' because He 'endured the cross, despising the shame'.

The noted Rabbi Duncan of Edinburgh once preached on the text 'he shall see His seed' (Is 53:10 AV). He divided the text as follows: (1) He shall see them born and brought in; (2) He shall see them educated and brought up; (3) He shall see them supported and brought through; (4) He shall see them glorified and brought home. This is part of the joy that was set before Him.

His return to earth will result in His eternal union with His Bride, the Church which He purchased with His own blood. For Him as for us, it will mean the ecstatic joy of the marriage supper of the Lamb, and eternal fellowship and communion.

When He returns it will be to receive the Kingdom of which He had so much to say when on earth. When He came to His own people and offered Himself as their King, their response was, 'We will not have this man to reign over us.' But at last His Kingship will be universally acknowledged and confessed.

> The Lord sits enthroned for ever, he has established his throne for judgement; and he judges the world with righteousness.
>
> Ps 9:7 RSV

> A day of righteous rule,
>   A day when Christ shall sway;
> A day when kings shall bow
>   And crowns before Him lay.

18
What the Second Advent Will Mean to Us

We can be absolutely certain that our Lord's second coming will result in our being completely changed into His own likeness, and the reception of resurrection bodies adapted to our new environment.

The prospect of the return of Christ should fill the believer who is walking in fellowship with Him with exultant joy.

Now we can only say, 'though you have not seen Him, you love Him, and though you do not see Him now, but believe in Him, you greatly rejoice with joy inexpressible and full of glory' (1 Pet 1:8). But then 'we shall see Him just as He is' (1 Jn 3:2). Faith will give place to sight, and when we see Him, 'we shall be like Him.' What a blessed transformation that will be when He 'will transform the body of our humble state into conformity with the body of His glory' (Phil 3:21). The transfiguration of our Lord gives some hint of what God can do with a human body.

> Behold, I tell you a mystery; we shall not all sleep, but we shall all be changed, in a moment, in the twinkling of an eye, at the last trumpet; for the trumpet will sound, and the dead will be raised imperishable, and we shall be changed.
>
> 1 Cor 15:51-52

The word 'moment' is the Greek word from which we get 'atom' and signifies the shortest possible fraction of time. The transformation will be instantaneous. No longer will our bodies be subject to decay, disease or death. Our mortal body will put on immortality.

It will be a time of joyous reunion with loved ones who have died 'in Christ'.

> The Lord Himself will descend from heaven...the dead in Christ shall rise first. Then we who are alive and remain shall be caught up together with them in the clouds to meet the Lord in the air, and thus we shall always be with the Lord.
> 1 Thess 4:16-17

The resurrection of Christ was the assurance of resurrection to every believer.

> For as in Adam all die, so also in Christ all shall be made alive. But each in his own order: Christ the first fruits, after that those who are Christ's at His coming.
> 1 Cor 15:22-23

It will be a time of perfected sanctification. Heb 10:14 asserts that 'by one offering He has perfected for all time those who are sanctified'. On earth this is a continuing process, but when He appears our sanctification and likeness to Christ will be complete.

> We know that, when He appears, we shall be like Him, because we shall see Him just as He is.
> 1 Jn 3:2

Oh, the bliss of being saved to sin no more! To be delivered not only from the power of sin but from its very presence! To have every longing after holiness and Christ-likeness fulfilled! Our Lord's purpose for every member of His Church is expressed in these words:

> That He might present to Himself the church in all her glory, having no spot or wrinkle or any such thing; but that she

THE SECOND ADVENT AND US

should be holy and blameless.

Eph 5:27

The second coming will mean that death is vanquished and we, like our Lord, will live in the power of an endless life. For those believers who are called upon to experience death, it is robbed of its sharpness and sting. To them it is not death but 'sleep', for resurrection is assured.

> If we believe that Jesus died and rose again, even so God will bring with Him those who have fallen asleep in Jesus.... For the Lord Himself will descend from heaven with a shout.
>
> 1 Thess 4:14-16

> We shall not all sleep, but we shall all be changed, in a moment...the dead will be raised imperishable...then will come about the saying that is written, 'Death is swallowed up in victory. O death, where is your victory? O death, where is your sting?'
>
> 1 Cor 15:51-55

For those who are alive when Christ returns, they too will enjoy a marvellous victory over death—not resurrection, but translation.

> We who are alive and remain shall be caught up together with them in the clouds to meet the Lord in the air, and thus we shall always be with the Lord.
>
> 1 Thess 4:17

19

What the Second Advent Will Mean to Satan

We can be absolutely certain that the second coming of our Lord will spell the eternal doom of Satan who from the beginning of creation has sought to thwart God's purposes of blessing for the human race.

The Scriptures foreshadow a tremendous climax to the conflict of the ages, to be ushered in by the second advent of Christ. For no created being will the second advent have greater significance than for the arch-enemy of God and man.

Since the time when Satan conspired to oust God from the throne of the universe but was himself ousted, he set up and directed a rival kingdom whose existence was acknowledged by the Lord.

> If...Satan also is divided against himself, how shall his kingdom stand?
>
> Lk 11:18

In contrast to the 'kingdom of God's beloved son', Satan's kingdom is designated 'the domain of darkness' (Col 1:13). Christ's Kingdom is so organized that His will is executed through angels to whom He has delegated authority to rule and serve under Him. Each rank of angels appears to have an assigned sphere and special responsibilities (Col 1:16).

In imitating the Kingdom of God, Satan organized his

THE SECOND ADVENT AND SATAN

kingdom of darkness along similar lines. He works through gradations of the demons who were involved in his fall from heavenly heights. It appears that some of these evil spirits have regional authority, e.g. 'the prince of Persia' and 'the prince of Greece' (Dan 10:13,20).

Scripture presents a consistent picture of these rival hierarchies as they wage warfare against His ancient people the Jews and later against Christ and His Church. Christ and all the good angels are concerned with securing man's eternal welfare. Satan and his evil demons are allied with evil men to effect man's eternal ruin.

At the end of the age Satan is seen in alliance with the beast and the false prophet, the three forming a sinister trinity of evil, united in their purpose to gain world dominion. The beast is apparently identical with the Antichrist:

> And I saw the beast and the kings of the earth and their armies, assembled to make war against Him who sat upon the horse, and against His army. And the beast was seized, and with him the false prophet...these two were thrown alive into the lake of fire which burns with brimstone.
>
> Rev 19:19-20

While on earth the Lord inflicted a stunning defeat on Satan first in the wilderness of temptation, and then on the cross. By His death He 'destroyed' (or, as the word means, 'brought to nought, rendered impotent') him that had the power of death, that is the devil. Describing this victory, Paul wrote,

> When He had disarmed the rulers and authorities, He made a public display of them, having triumphed over them through Him.
>
> Col 2:15

John adds,

> The Son of Man appeared for this purpose, that He might destroy the works of the devil.
>
> 1 Jn 3:8

These and many other passages attest the stunning defeat inflicted on Satan at the cross. There the victory was gained and the sentence of doom was passed. It was there, too, that the Seed of the woman bruised and mortally wounded Satan's head, though He had His heel bruised in the conflict.

Since Calvary, the vaunted power of the adversary is only temporary, an empty show. He is bound but, as a preacher once quaintly put it, he is bound with a rather loose rope! For purposes which in God's sight are wise and good, He has allowed Satan a limited freedom; but for him the second advent of Christ will be the beginning of the end. Then it will be seen that his power is not inherent but delegated by God; that it is not invincible, but shattered (Lk 11:21-22); that it is not triumphant, but doomed (Rev 20:2-3). He and his accomplices are reserved for a last judgement that is still future.

Concerning the problem of the liberty God has granted to Satan, Dr L. S. Chafer wrote: 'Though the day of execution is, in the purpose of God delayed, it is nevertheless sure, and the day is fast approaching when an awful destruction of self-enthroned beings will be executed.... It would seem that Satan cherishes the expectation of accomplishing his purpose until near the end of his career.' (Rev 12:7-12.)

The universal prevalence of lawlessness, violence and immorality and the widespread revival of the occult indicates that the devil, realizing that his time is short, is doing all he can to postpone the execution of the sentence passed on him at the cross.

THE SECOND ADVENT AND SATAN

> Woe to the earth and the sea; because the devil has come down to you, having great wrath, knowing that he has only a short time.
>
> Rev 12:12

'The inconceivable patience of God with regard to Satan and humanity shall, however, have an end,' wrote Dr Rene Pache. 'The Lord will take again the government of the world which He has provisionally handed to the hands of the nations and the usurper.' (*The Return of Jesus Christ*, p. 168.)

The description of Satan's final overthrow and doom and the complete and utter defeat of his hellish strategy is accomplished with a great economy of words. But there is about it an awesome and reassuring finality:

> And when the thousand years are completed, Satan will be released from his prison, and will come out to deceive the nations...to gather them together for the war.... And the devil who deceived them was thrown into the lake of fire and brimstone, where the beast and the false prophet are also; and they will be tormented day and night forever and ever.
>
> Rev 20:7-8, 10

20
Practical Effects of the Doctrine

We can be absolutely certain that loving the appearing of Christ will provide powerful motivation for holy living and zealous service.

'Hope and belief in the second coming of the Lord, the knowledge that He is coming again, is something meant to sustain us in trial, to strengthen us in weakness, to solace us in mourning, to stir us up to service. It is something that explains the past and cheers the present and promises perfection in the future. The second coming of the Lord Jesus Christ is, and is meant to be, a continuous power in the minds of those who know and believe in Him as the One who died for our sins and rose again for our justification.' (Hubert Brooke, *The Keswick Week*, Marshalls 1910, p. 110.)

Both Scripture and Christian experience combine to show that this doctrine is nothing if not practical in its application. It has rightly been contended that there is hardly any second advent text in the New Testament that does not in itself or in its context insist upon the influence such a hope ought to have on our inner spiritual life or on the mood of our soul.

It is set forth as an incentive to holy living

> And now, little children, abide in Him, so that when He appears, we may have confidence and not shrink away from Him in shame at His coming.
>
> 1 Jn 2:28

We know that, when He appears, we shall be like Him, because we shall see Him just as He is. And every one who has this hope fixed on Him purifies himself, just as He is pure.

1 Jn 3:2-3

It is unfortunate that so much emphasis has been given by exponents of this truth to its speculative and sensational side and so little to its ethical implications, for it is bound up with so many practical exhortations to Christian patience, obligation and attainment.

Be patient, therefore, brethren, until the coming of the Lord.... You too be patient...for the coming of the Lord is at hand.

Jas 5:7-8

The grace of God has appeared...instructing us to deny ungodliness and worldly desires and to live sensibly, righteously and godly in the present age, looking for the blessed hope and the appearing of the glory of our great God and Savior, Christ Jesus....

Tit 2:11-13

The testimonies of notable Christians of the past to the practical and transforming effects of this doctrine are given, in the hope that they will have a similar effect on those who read them.

Effect on Bible Study. Arthur T. Pierson, one of the most profound Bible students of his day, wrote: 'When I found this truth, I began to discover what I had not seen before, that it is the pivot of every epistle of the New Testament. Two-thirds of the Bible which had been sealed to me were opened by this key, and I was permitted to enter and walk through the marvellous chambers of mystery.' (Quoted in J. O. Sanders, *The Incomparable Christ*, pp. 254-55.)

Effect on missionary motivation. Dr Pierson was also a great missionary statesman and editor of the *Missionary Review of the World.* Concerning the effect of the second advent on his missionary motivation he wrote: 'From the day when I first saw the hope of our Lord's return as imminent, new courage came into my soul, and new iron into my blood, and I have been labouring under the divinely inspired expectation of the successful completion of Christ's body, the Church.' (Sanders, pp. 254-55.)

Effect on Christian experience. The Rev. W. Hewitson, a godly preacher, declared that the discovery of the scriptural hope of our Lord's second coming wrought in him a change amounting almost to a second conversion.

Effect on soul-winning. George Müller, that mighty man of prayer, testified of the effect the discovery of this doctrine produced in him: 'From my inmost soul I was stirred up to feel compassion for perishing sinners, and for the slumbering world lying in the wicked one. Ought I not to do all I can to win souls for the sleeping church? I determined to go from place to place to preach the gospel and arouse the church to look and wait for the second advent of our Lord from heaven. For fifty-two years my heart has been true to these two points.' (Sanders, pp. 254-55.)

Effect on evangelical conviction. Dr A. J. Gordon, brilliant Bible teacher and pastor, affirmed: 'The discovery of this primitive doctrine of the gospel constituted a new era in my study of the Word of God, and gave the opening-out into vistas of truth hitherto undreamed of. And moreover, it was the means of the deepest and firmest anchoring in all the doctrines of the evangelical faith. I confess myself so indebted to this hope in every way, that I cannot measure the loss it would have been to have passed through my ministry without the knowledge of it.' (Quoted in A. T. Pierson, *How Christ Came to Church*, Baptist Book Society 1895, p. 27.)

Effect on hope. J. Wilbur Chapman, who circled the globe in fruitful evangelistic ministry, wrote: 'The truth of our Lord's pre-millennial return has worked out in my life in a very practical and helpful way. It has increased my desire to serve Him. It has given me an optimistic spirit concerning the advancement of the cause of Christ, and it has given me an ever-increasing joy in preaching.' (Sanders, pp. 254-55.)

Effect on preparedness. J. Hudson Taylor, founder of the China Inland Mission (now the Overseas Missionary Fellowship), wrote: 'Well do I remember the effect when God was pleased to open my heart to the great truth that the Lord Jesus was coming again, and might come at any time. Since He might come any day, it is well to be ready every day. I do not know of any truth that has been a greater blessing to me through life than this.' (Sanders, pp. 254-55.)

Dr G. Campbell Morgan bore this testimony to the effect this doctrine had on his outlook on life: 'To me the second coming is the perpetual light on the path which makes the present bearable. I never lay my head on the pillow without thinking that before I awake the final day may have dawned. I never begin my work without thinking that He may interrupt it and begin His work.' (Quoted in J. Wesley White, *Re-Entry,* Zondervan 1970, p. 175.)

21
Our Attitude to Christ's Return

We can be absolutely certain that a lack of expectancy of Christ's return will impoverish our spiritual life here, and rob us of reward in the life to come.

If, as has been shown, the Scripture writers with one united voice assert that Christ is returning to this earth, then we should seriously examine our own attitude in the light of this momentous event. To one who did not know the subtlety of his own heart, it would seem that only one attitude would be possible to a follower of Christ—eager expectation. But this is far from the truth.

'Strange to say,' wrote Ruth Paxson, 'there are four very evident attitudes manifested in the professing Church towards this blessed hope; aggressive hostility, listless apathy, fearful apprehension, and loving expectancy. Some hate it; some are totally ignorant of it; some are afraid of it; and some love it.' (*Life on the Highest Plane,* vol. 3, Moody Press 1928, p. 287.)

Scripture gives clear teaching on this subject.

We are to love His appearing, which will be a time of reward for faithful service.

> In the future there is laid up for me the crown of righteousness, which the Lord, the righteous Judge, will award to me on that day; and not only to me, but also to all who have loved His appearing.
>
> 2 Tim 4:8

Can we say that we love His appearing? Are our affections centred on the One who is coming?

We are to look for and earnestly desire His advent.

> The day of the Lord will come like a thief, in which the heavens will pass away with a roar and the elements will be destroyed with intense heat.... Since all these things are to be destroyed in this way, what sort of people ought you to be in holy conduct and godliness, looking for and hastening the coming of the day of God....
>
> 2 Pet 3:10-12

It is true that terrible judgements lie ahead for a world that has rejected the mercy and salvation of God when Christ returns. Only the wilfully blind can fail to see that. But God's eternal purpose includes the final vanquishing of Satan and his hosts of evil, and the establishing of new heavens and a new earth wherein righteousness dwells. The believer looks with eager eyes to see the rightful King on His throne.

The most frequent exhortation in connection with the Lord's coming is that we should be on the alert. The warnings and exhortations of Christ and His apostles seem to indicate that many Christians will be caught unawares and unprepared because of their lack of interest. Hence the oft-repreated command,

> The coming of the Son of Man will be just like the days of Noah.... Therefore be on the alert, for you do not know which day your Lord is coming.
>
> Mt 24:37, 42

> 'What I say to you I say to all, "Be on the alert!"'
>
> Mk 13:37

> You yourselves know full well that the day of the Lord will come just like a thief in the night...so then let us not sleep as others do, but let us be alert and sober.
>
> 1 Thess 5:2, 6

On the day of His return we will be engaged in our ordinary tasks. No warning will be given, any more than a thief gives advance notice of his intended theft. There will be no time for special preparation, so we must be on the alert and ready to welcome Him every day.

In one of His parables of the second advent, Jesus urged His disciples to *emulate the businessman* in their stewardship of the gospel.

> A certain nobleman went to a distant country to receive a kingdom for himself, and then return. And he called ten of his slaves, and gave them ten minas [equal to about 100 day's wages], and said to them, 'Do business with this until I come back.'
>
> Lk 19:12-13

In his zeal to make a profit with the capital at his disposal, the businessman gives himself without reservation to his trading. So is it to be with the Lord's followers. They are to be gripped by a passion to spread the gospel which has been entrusted to them by their Master, a passion which will not abate until the glorious message is carried to every creature.

Another repeated exhortation is that we are to *await the return of Christ from heaven.*

> Be dressed in readiness, and keep your lamps alight. And be like men who are waiting for their master when he returns....
> Lk 12:35-36

> So that you are not lacking in any gift, awaiting eagerly the revelation of our Lord Jesus Christ.
>
> 1 Cor 1:7

> You turned to God from idols to serve a living and true God, and to wait for His Son from heaven.
>
> 1 Thess 1:9-10

It would be possible to wait for a coming event listlessly and indifferently, but the force of the verb 'wait' is 'to look forward with patience and confidence'. When we await a loved friend who is coming to visit us, we have made adequate provision for his arrival and arranged our activities so that we can extend to him a worthy welcome. Much more should we do so for our coming Lord. It is like the waiting of a bride for the coming of her bridegroom.

The final exhortation in connection with the second advent is to *hold fast what we have.*

> Nevertheless what you have, hold fast until I come.
>
> Rev 2:25

> I am coming quickly; hold fast what you have, in order that no one take your crown.
>
> Rev 3:11

The relevance of this command in our day of widespread apostasy needs no emphasis. In loyalty to our coming Lord, we are to hold tenaciously the deposit of truth entrusted to our care. The verb means 'to take a firm grip on'. Alford suggests that what the believers had and were to hold fast to was 'the sum total of Christian doctrine and hope and privilege'. Failure to hold these fast will involve forfeiture of the crown of reward.

22

Heaven – Our Home

We can be absolutely certain that our Lord will fulfil His promise to come again and receive us to Himself to live for ever in the glorious heaven He has prepared for His children.

> In My Father's house are many dwelling places; if it were not so, I would have told you; for I go to prepare a place for you. And if I go and prepare a place for you, I will come again, and receive you to Myself; that where I am, there you may be also.
> Jn 14:2-3

The second coming of our Lord will, as He said, mean for us the beginning of the glories of heaven—the home He has gone to prepare for us. While there is much about heaven that is mysterious, sufficient has been revealed in Scripture to make our hearts thrill with eager anticipation. The problem of expressing the infinite to finite beings led God to use symbol and metaphor to convey the truth.

Strangely enough, most of what we know about heaven is negative. We know far more about the things that are absent from heaven than the things that are present. And the things that are absent are, in the main, the things that cause us most pain and distress in our earthly environment.

The word 'heaven' means 'that which is above'. The word is used in the Bible in a threefold sense—the atmospheric heavens, the celestial or starry heavens, and the abode of the Holy Trinity. 'His throne is in the heavens': heaven is where God is. It is a home where there will be loving companionship and joyous service. For His bride, Christ is preparing not servants' quarters, but a bridal suite.

Absentees from heaven

In preparing this eternal home for us, our ascended Lord removes all that would spoil our enjoyment or cast gloom on our spirits. What will be absent from heaven?

Tears. 'And He shall wipe away every tear from their eyes' (Rev 21:4). God will take heaven's handkerchief and wipe away tears caused by sin, failure, pain, sorrow and bereavement.

Death. 'And there shall no longer be any death' (Rev 21:4). The 'king of terrors' and the 'last enemy' will never be able to enter the pearly gates. No longer will we be 'through fear of death subject to bondage'. Christ extracted the sting from death by His death and resurrection, but now it is for ever banished from the universe. 'And death and Hades were thrown into the lake of fire' (20:14).

Mourning. 'And...there shall no longer be any mourning, or crying' (Rev 21:4)—because of the ravages of sin or the poignancy of bereavement.

Pain. 'And...there shall no longer be any...pain' (Rev 21:4). The worst thing about illness for both the patient and the onlookers is often the excruciating pain that accompanies it. '...The whole creation groans and suffers the pains of childbirth together until now' (Rom 8:22), but in heaven there will be no need of the painkilling drugs that are so welcome to suffering humanity.

Sickness. 'And he showed me a river of the water of life' clear as crystal.... And on either side of the river was the tree of life...and the leaves of the tree were for the healing of the nations' (Rev 22:1-2). When Jesus returns, no believer will ever again toss on a sick bed.

Hunger. 'They shall hunger no more' (Rev 7:16). In the year of writing it is estimated that as many as 400 million in Africa, Asia and Latin America are likely to suffer starvation. In heaven there is no more hunger or thirst.

Night. 'And there shall no longer be any night' (Rev 22:5). What a blessing night is to the animal and vegetable world—the time of rest and renewal. But in heaven the body will no longer be in need of this recuperative process, for we will experience neither fatigue nor exhaustion.

Temple. 'And I saw no temple in it, for the Lord God, the Almighty, and the Lamb, are its temple' (Rev 21:22). Buildings set apart for worship will no longer be necessary, for we will dwell in the immediate presence of God.

Curse. 'And there shall no longer be any curse' (Rev 22:3). The Bible ends where it began. Our first parents were expelled from the garden with its river and the tree of life, and had a curse pronounced on them. Through our Saviour's cross the curse has been removed, and we live for ever in the eternal city with its crystal river and its tree of life.

Positive characteristics of heaven

The following will characterize our heavenly home:

Glory. 'I desire that they also, whom Thou has given Me,

be with Me where I am...that they may behold My glory (Jn 17:24). 'And the city has no need of the sun or of the moon to shine upon it, for the glory of God has illumined it' (Rev 21:23).

Holiness. 'I dwell on a high and holy place' (Is 57:15). 'And nothing unclean and no one who practices abomination and lying, shall ever come into it' (Rev 21:27).

Beauty. 'Out of Zion, the perfection of beauty, God has shone forth' (Ps 50:2). In heaven every aesthetic desire and aspiration will find complete satisfaction.

Light. 'The Lord God shall illimine them' (Rev 22:5). God dwells in light unapproachable by man in his earthly state, but it will not be so in heaven. 'The Lord God shall illumine them...they shall not have need of the light of a lamp nor the light of the sun.'

Unity. In heaven the Lord's prayer in the upper room will be answered. 'I do not ask in behalf of these alone; but for those also who believe in Me through their word; that they may all be one...just as We are one' (Jn 17:20-22). All will be harmony and unity akin to that which exists between the members of the Godhead.

Perfection. 'We know in part...but when the perfect comes, the partial will be done away with' (1 Cor 13:9-10). Paul expressed his assurance of future perfection: 'For I am confident of this very thing, that He who began a good work in you will perfect it until the day of Christ Jesus' (Phil 1:6). In heaven we will attain to full maturity.

Joy. The climate of heaven is one of unalloyed joy—'joy unspeakable and full of glory.' 'In Thy presence is fulness of joy; In Thy right hand there are pleasures forever' (Ps 16:11).

Love. Love is a perennial flower whose petals never fall. 'But now abide faith, hope, love, these three; but the greatest of these is love' (1 Cor 13:13).

Satisfaction. 'I will be satisfied with Thy likeness when I awake' (Ps 17:15). In heaven no holy desire or aspiration will remain unsatisfied.

The activities of heaven

Few have any clear idea as to how the saints will be occupied in heaven, and there is indeed much that remains unrevealed in this area. But we know that these four activities will engage us.

Worship and adoration. We will take delight in paying to God the worship and adoration that is His due. 'The twenty-four elders'—representative of all redeemed humanity—'will fall down before Him who sits on the throne, and will worship Him who lives forever and ever, and will cast their crowns before the throne, saying, "Worthy art Thou, our Lord and our God, to receive glory and honor and power"' (Rev 4:10-11).

Music holds a prominent place in the imagery of heaven, as it did in the worship of tabernacle and temple. 1 Chronicles 25:1-8 tells us that there were 288 musicians employed in the temple service. Both vocal and instrumental music are cited as adding to the felicity of heaven. 'And they sang a new song' (Rev 5:9). 'The twenty-four elders fell down before the Lamb, having each one a harp' (5:8). If earthly choirs and orchestras can lift us to such heights of enjoyment, what must the music of heaven be like?

Fellowship. On earth there are few things that are more beautiful than the fellowship enjoyed by kindred spirits. In heaven with all causes of dissension and discord excluded we shall enjoy a glorious extension of fellowship with the saints on earth. And we have time and leisure to cultivate new friendships with the saints of all ages.

Service. 'For this reason, they are before the throne of God; and they serve Him day and night in His temple' (Rev 7:15). 'And His bond-servants shall serve Him' (22:3). We will then have bodies like Christ's and will know none of the limitations of time and space we now experience. In six millennia we have only begun to explore the wonders of our own planet. What endless vistas of possibility open up as we think of ceaseless service for the Omnipotent God throughout the whole of His vast universe.

Our Lord made it clear that in the heavenly state there will be degrees of responsibility delegated to His servants as a reward for faithfulness in service on earth. 'And He said to him... "be in authority over ten cities." And the second came.... And he said to him also, "And you are to be over five cities"' (Lk 19:17-19).

Reunion with loved ones. The question is constantly asked, 'Will we know one another in heaven?' If this were not so, heaven would be a retrograde step. There we will know more, not less. We shall know even as we are known. We should bear in mind that the essential element in personality is not the body but the spirit, and there is no indication in Scripture that any relationship of our spiritual life will be destroyed.

Mary recognized the risen Christ by His voice when He said, 'Mary!' The disciples on the Emmaus road recognized the risen Christ at table. In our Lord's parable in Luke 16 the rich man, Abraham, and Lazarus are represented as recognizing each other. Peter, James, and John knew Moses and Elijah on the Mount of Transfiguration.

In heaven every holy and spiritual relationship of earth will apparently continue in purified form. Pure and holy love between believers in this life is the creation of God and God does not destroy what He has created. Family relations—husband and wife, parents and child, brother and sister—are not broken.

But there is one significant change. In replying to the captious criticism of the Sadducees, Jesus said:

> Those who are considered worthy to attain to that age and the resurrection from the dead, neither marry, nor are given in marriage; for neither can they die any more, for they are like angels, and are sons of God, being sons of the resurrection.
>
> Lk 20:35-36

In the heavenly life conjugal relations are not the same, for there is no death; there is no longer the need for procreation for the continuance of the human race. All will be immortal.

But it should be borne in mind that the joys of heaven are open only to those whose names are written in the Lamb's book of life. How important, then, to be *absolutely sure* that our names are so recorded.